Muir Ramble Route

Mar 27, 1868 arrived SF (age 30)
~ may 22   Yosemite Valley

Muir Ramble Route

Walking from San Francisco to Yosemite
In the Footsteps of John Muir

A Guide for hiking from San Francisco to Yosemite by
Peter and Donna Thomas

With an account of the original 1868 trip by
John Muir

Poetic Matrix Press

Photos, unless credited, are by Peter and Donna Thomas.

Front Cover photo: Old Big Oak Flat Road, Yosemite

Back Cover Photo: Near Pacheco Pass

Title page photo: Fields Road, Snelling

Acknowledgement is made for permission to reproduce the following: All of John Muir's letters and writing not in public domain appear courtesy of the John Muir Papers, Holt-Atherton Department of Special Collections, University of the Pacific Libraries. Copyright 1984 Muir-Hanna Trust.

ISBN: 978-0-9824276-6-8

First Revision
Second Revision

Poetic Matrix Press
PO Box 1223
Madera, CA 93639
www.poeticmatrix.com

Preface

Both Donna and I grew up next to open spaces. We spent much of our early childhoods outdoors, hiking, exploring, wading in creeks, climbing in trees and over rocks. Donna's parents were Scout leaders and she grew up backpacking, my parents took me surfing. To be really honest, as a kid I watched my share of TV. We are both just regular folks. Throughout our lives we have continued to backpack, camp and be in love with the outdoors, in fact Donna has hiked the John Muir Trail twice, but we did not grow up to be professional adventurers, biologists or naturalists. We ended up as book artists. I make paper and have an old letterpress with lots of metal type. Donna uses pen and watercolors to paint words and images. Together we create one-of-a-kind and limited edition books. We know how to make artist's books, but found writing this guidebook a challenge and have many people to thank:

Thank you to the many John Muir scholars who helped us with the research including: Bonnie Gisel, Harold Wood, Bob Bouer and Howard Cooley.

Thank you to all the libraries and librarians including Charlene Duval and San Jose's MLK Library, Shan Sutton and UOP's Holt Atherton Library, Gary Kurutz and the California State Library, the California Academy of Sciences, the Northern Mariposa County Historical Museum, Merced's Courthouse Museum, Los Banos' Milliken Museum and the Gustine Historical Museum.

Thank you to those who have helped with the text including: Sam Eastman, Gary Young, Nick Gravem at Down Works, Bob Fenster, Julia Callahan, Alex McInturff, Toby Weinert, Boyd Cothran, and Polly Goldman.

Thank you to those who gave us encouragement and support during and after the walk including: The Book Club of California, Patagonia, Roslyn Bullas of Wilderness Press, Malcolm Margolin of Heyday Books, and Carl Hall of the San Francisco Chronicle.

When people hear that we walked from San Francisco to Yosemite they are usually amazed that it is actually possible and the first question is always, "How far is it and how many pairs of shoes did you wear out?" It was 300 miles but only took one pair of shoes. We are not super athletes and this trek is something any average physically fit person can do. We hope that this book will inspire "the adventurer" in every reader to get up, get out, and follow the footsteps of John Muir to Yosemite.

Peter Thomas

Rainbow View, Yosemite

Contents

Cream cups

Crossing the Cascade Creek Bridge

Muir Ramble Route

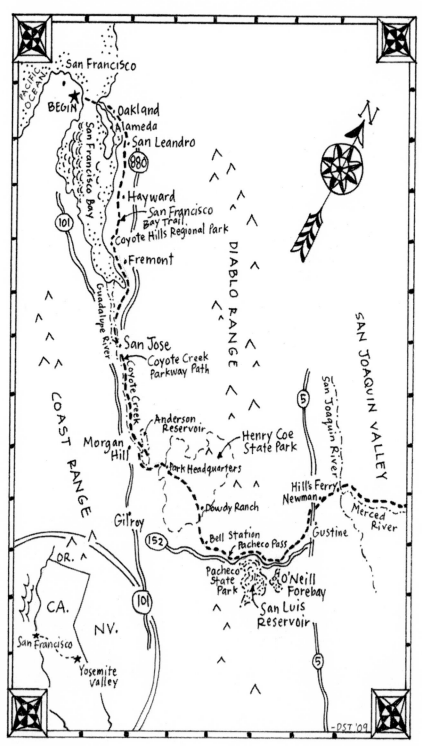

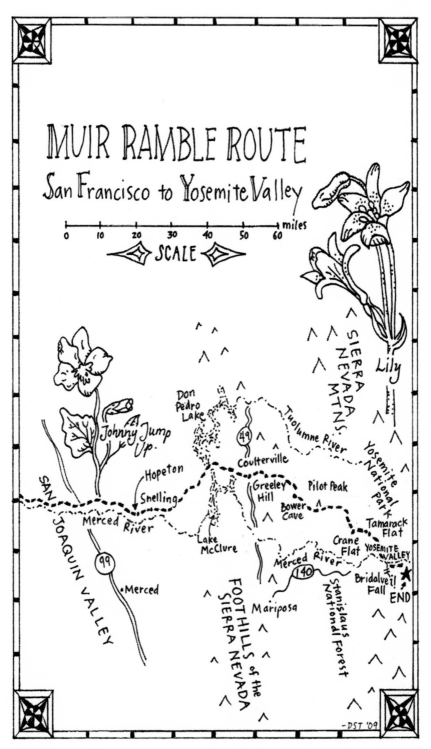

MUIR RAMBLE ROUTE
San Francisco to Yosemite Valley

miles

0   10   20   30   40   50   60

SCALE

Lily

Johnny Jump Up.

SIERRA NEVADA MTNS.

Don Pedro Lake

Tuolumne River

49

Coulterville

Yosemite National Park

Hopeton

Greeley Hill

Pilot Peak

Snelling

Bower Cave

Tamarack Flat

Merced River

SAN JOAQUIN VALLEY

Lake McClure

Crane Flat

YOSEMITE VALLEY

99

Merced River

140

Bridalveil Fall

END

Merced

Stanislaus National Forest

FOOT HILLS of the SIERRA NEVADA

Mariposa

-DST '09

Introduction

In the early morning of March 28, 1868, twenty-nine year old John Muir stepped off the crowded steamship "Nebraska" into the busy San Francisco waterfront. He had just arrived from New York, via Panama, had been cooped up on the ship with a "barbarous mob" for much too long, and was ready to "get to the uncultivated wild part of the state." He asked the first person he encountered for directions and then set off on what would be a six week long, three hundred mile trip across California to Yosemite.

In 1868 John Muir was just another of the many thousands of hopeful immigrants and curious visitors who have arrived in California hoping to make their fortune or have the opportunity to see the natural wonders of the state. Today he is internationally recognized as a founder of the Sierra Club, the man who talked President Roosevelt into making Yosemite a National Park and a prominent figure in the development of the modern environmental and conservation movements. He is also the man on the California quarter and he is there for a good reason. Like Washington and Lincoln, he was a hero.

John Muir was an explorer, a feel-no-pain adventurer, a hardcore mountaineer, and a deeply religious man who ecstatically saw God in all nature. Today he is a role model for people who love nature and the outdoors. Anyone who has hiked in the Sierra has probably heard the story about how he would just grab a loaf of bread, put a few bags of tea in his pocket, throw a coat over his shoulder and head off into the Sierra. In this era of urban sprawl and mega-highways crisscrossing the landscape, it is an amazing, almost magical thing to ponder: that a person could walk across California to Yosemite.

Even in 1868, the year before the completion of the transcontinental railroad, Yosemite, with its immense granite cliffs, huge waterfalls and giant trees, was already a tourist destination. The first travel guide to Yosemite, *"Scenes of Wonder and Curiosity in California"* was published in 1862. In it the author, James M. Hutchings, describes Yosemite as a "wonder of the world", a place to see before you die. Hutchings even details the best route to get there from San Francisco, advising the reader to take the ferry to Stockton, a stage to Coulterville, and then enter the Yosemite Valley on horseback.

Muir did not follow Hutchings' advice. He walked. As Muir wrote: [1] "…we had plenty of time, and proposed drifting leisurely mountainward, via the valley of San Jose, Pacheco Pass, and the plain of San Joaquin, and thence to Yosemite by any road that we chanced to find; enjoying the flowers and light, 'camping out' in our blankets wherever overtaken by night, and paying very little compliance to roads or times." He started the trip by taking a ferry to Oakland, and soon found nature in abundance. Muir wrote: "We proceeded up the Santa Clara Valley to San Jose. It was the bloom-time of the year. The landscapes were fairly drenched with sunshine, all the air was quivering with the songs of the meadow-larks, and the hills were so covered with flowers that they seemed to be painted. Slow indeed was my progress through these glorious gardens, the first of the California flora I had seen."[2]

Following John Muir's Footsteps

In the summer of 2005 Donna was backpacking the John Muir Trail (JMT) the 212-mile hiking route, named in Muir's honor, which travels along the crest of California's Sierra Nevada mountain range from Yosemite Valley to Mt. Whitney. Donna was with a bunch of friends, Katy Sommer, David Worton, Tom Killion, and Jean Paul Cane, who are all veteran backpackers. They would hike and talk for hours, telling stories and making plans for future hikes. One day, just on the way out of Evolution Basin towards Muir Pass, talk turned to backpacking gear and food. Jean Paul said, "You know, John Muir would just grab a loaf of bread, put some tea in his pocket, throw a coat over his shoulder and walk to Yosemite…" It's the story we all have heard before. This time Donna heard something more in it, maybe it was a call from Muir in the wind whispering down the pass, and she said to everyone, "I want to do that. I'm going to step out my door and walk to Yosemite."

When Donna got home she told me what she had decided to do. I surprised her by saying that I wanted to go too. I say surprised, because even though we had enjoyed camping and backpacking together, I preferred surfing to hiking, and had rarely shown interest in long distance walking or walking for pleasure. But this idea: to walk across California, to walk in John Muir's footsteps, it intrigued me. It intrigued us both. Would it still be possible to get to Yosemite on foot? Donna felt sure it was and vowed to find someone who had already done it and mapped out the route. We could then leave on the trip the next spring. But we could not find anyone who had ever re-traced Muir's 1868 trek to Yosemite. We had often driven to Yosemite, and knew what the trip was like in a car. We wondered what it would be like to walk: what we would see and experience as we took the trip at a human pace.

In six months we had gathered enough information to determine Muir's actual route. What we found was a bit discouraging: the little dirt roads Muir had followed in 1868 were now mostly paved roads, busy city streets or highways. But by this time we were committed to walking in Muir's footsteps. Donna said to me, "Lets just go ahead and do it, even if it means walking on asphalt. We can just take our time, go slowly, look closely, use "John Muir's eyes" to see California and appreciate nature the way he did, and have a good time doing it."

We took that trip in 2006. Walking with Muir as our guide we began to see things differently than we would have without him. We began to see the grandeur of nature in small open spaces. In Muir's day there was so much open space it was hard for the average person to see the need to set aside land as wilderness. Visionary that he was, Muir lobbied tirelessly for the creation of a national park system to preserve the wilderness. We reap the benefit of that work every time we visit places like Yosemite or the Sierra Nevada backcountry.

Today it is equally hard for many people to see a need for preserving what open space still remains in urban, suburban and rural California, or any need to create routes for travel between those spaces without the use of a car. But the need is there. Making this evident is the challenge of our day. Speaking to this in *"The Practice of the Wild"*, Gary Snyder wrote: "The point (of a wilderness experience) is to make intimate contact with the real world, real self... Inspiration, exaltation, and insight do not end when one steps outside the doors of the church. The wilderness as temple is only a beginning. One should … be able to come back to the lowlands and see all the land about us, agricultural, suburban, urban, as part of the same territory — never totally ruined, never completely unnatural."[3] By honoring the nature in the lowlands, by setting aside open spaces and creating right of ways and trails, we have the opportunity to do the same favor for those of our future that Muir and other early environmentalists did for us.

With Muir as our guide we also saw how much California has changed since 1868. Back then California had few people, few buildings and very few roads. Those roads helped the traveler on foot, horseback or stage to cross a mostly undeveloped landscape. Today there are many more roads and there is much less open space. The irony is now it's actually harder to walk across California than it was a hundred years ago. Freeways, private property and lack of accommodations spaced and placed for walking have made it almost impossible for the self-powered adventurer to travel any long distance legally. This book is about reclaiming the right and the freedom to walk. It is about preserving open space and creating trails. It is about making a positive change in the world. It is about following John Muir's footsteps on a self-powered vacation, an "urban backpacking" trip from the San Francisco Bay Area to Yosemite.

How the book is structured

The book is divided into four parts.

Part One tells the story of John Muir's 1868 trip from San Francisco to Yosemite in his own words. John Muir wrote about the trip, but never as a separate book, so the story had remained obscure and hidden in a tangle of literary sources. We created this text by compiling everything Muir wrote about the trip into a single unified account. More than just describing the route, it presents 1868 California from John Muir's point of view, describing unlikely places like the Santa Clara Valley with the same religious fervor that he later used when writing about Yosemite. By publishing this account we now make available to the general reader what had previously only been available to a handful of Muir scholars.

In Part Two we first describe Muir's route in relationship to the roads that exist today. We then describe our discovery and creation of a route to walk in his footsteps. It turns out that most of the roads Muir walked are now paved over and many are major highways, unsafe or unpleasant for walking. Our new route, the Muir Ramble Route, (MRR), stays near to, but does not always follow those roads. It wanders a little to the left or a little to the right in an attempt to go where Muir would have gone if he were walking with us today: anywhere that is wild, places where nature can still be found.

Part Three is the guidebook for following the 300-mile Muir Ramble Route from San Francisco to Yosemite. Directions are given for the complete trip. Since most readers will not be able to follow the whole route as a single "through hike" trip the directions are divided into seven regional sections and each section has a Recommended Trip that can be completed over a long weekend. Some of these trips are best done on foot, others may be more fun when riding on a bicycle, and these options are discussed in the guidebook. Additionally, highlights from the trips we have taken following the MRR are printed in sidebars with the directions.

In Part Four we share some of our thoughts about what can be done to help create a healthy environment. We also present our vision for the future: one where it is possible to leave the car behind and walk or ride a bike, following the Muir Ramble Route from the Bay Area to Yosemite as a "green" or "self-powered" vacation. We then suggest some things you can do to help make this vision for the MRR a reality.

Part One:
John Muir's First Trip to Yosemite

What follows is the story of John Muir's 1868 walk from San Francisco to Yosemite. It is interesting to think that John Muir might never have come to California if he hadn't had an accident. In 1867, working in a wagon wheel factory in Indianapolis, he pierced his right eye with an awl and both eyes went blind. Muir, whose passion at this time was botany, vowed that if he did recover his sight he would not return to work on his mechanical inventions, but would travel the world and "devote the rest of my life to the study of the inventions of God."[1]

His eyesight improved and he set off walking to the Gulf of Mexico with the intention to go on to South America, to the source of the Amazon, where he would build a raft and float to the Atlantic. But Muir contracted malaria in Florida and changed his plans. "I decided to visit California for a year or two, to see its wonderful flora and the famous Yosemite Valley. All the world was before me and every day was a holiday, so it did not seem important to which one of the world's wildernesses I first should wander."[2]

Documenting Muir's trip

John Muir wrote many books: tales of his adventures in the wilderness and stories of his life and his observations of nature. Muir foresaw the need to preserve wilderness and books like *My First Summer In the Sierra* were published in part to further that end. Muir's 1868 botanical ramble is not the story of an epic adventure in the wilderness, but rather the story of a walk to get to the wilderness. In the not so recent past this was not a story many people were interested in: there was still plenty of open space in California; the roads were not full of cars, nor were they unappealing and unsafe places to walk. Perhaps that explains why it was overlooked: it wasn't much of a story. But things have changed. Now when someone walks from San Francisco to Yosemite it is front page news. Today Californians need alternatives to automotive transportation and more pleasant and picturesque places to walk. The time has come for Muir's story to be told, to give the inspiration to create places to walk in and between our local communities.

Muir mentions his 1868 trip in fourteen different literary sources.[3] Each text was composed for a particular reason, and described the trip from a different perspective. For example, in the magazine article *Rambles of a Botanist* Muir focuses on the flora, while in his book *The Yosemite*, Muir is concerned with the landscape. This made it hard to grasp the complete story of the trip. We could see that if the accounts were combined they would create an interesting new chronicle of this formative time in Muir's life, before he found his spiritual home in Yosemite.

To create this account we took all of Muir's texts, sorted them by region (i.e. San Francisco Bay area, Pacheco Pass, etc.), then recombined them into one seamless narrative that is written in the form of a letter, one that John Muir might have written to a friend or family member shortly after finishing his trip to Yosemite. In this imagined letter, Muir first reflects on the trip as a whole, then gives the details of his trip from San Francisco to Yosemite, and concludes with a plea to come visit California, saying, "Yo Semite alone is worth the expense and danger of any journey in the world."[4]

The major sources for this text were books and magazine articles that are in the public domain, but some information came from unpublished letters, and these were used with permission from the copyright holders. As duplicate passages were merged to create this unified account, the goal was to make as few changes to his original words as possible. Occasionally the word order or sentence structure was changed, as were the tense or case when they no longer matched, and very occasionally a word had to be inserted for clarity. The text is footnoted, listing the source material for each paragraph. When the text was made by combining sources, the primary source is listed first, the secondary source listed second and so on.

For those interested in reading the original source material, John Muir's books can be found in most reference libraries. Additional materials, including original letters and personal artifacts, are held in archives at the University of Wisconsin in Madison and the University of the Pacific (UOP) in Stockton, California. The collection at UOP contains all of his original diaries and journals. UOP has journals for both his 1867 thousand-mile walk and the 1869 first summer in the Sierra, but no journal for the 1868 ramble across California. Were there a journal, or had Muir written a book about this trip, as he did of the trips taken in 1867 or 1869, this botanical ramble to Yosemite would be well known today. We hope that with this telling, the story will become more widely known.

Donna in the UC Berkeley Map Library

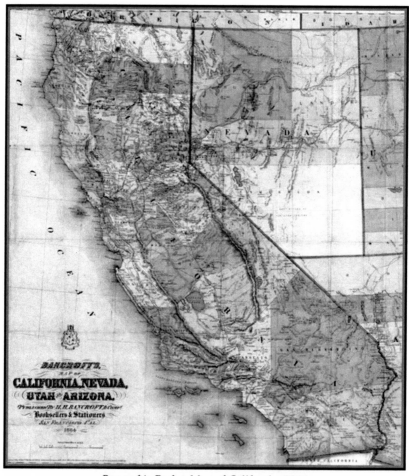

Bancroft's Pocket Map of California, 1864
David Rumsey Map Collection, www.davidrumsey.com

The Story of John Muir's 1868 Trip from San Francisco to Yosemite

[Dear Friends,]

Fate and flowers carried me to California, and I have reveled and luxuriated amid its mountains and plants and bright sky. I followed the Diablo foothills along the San José Valley to Gilroy, thence over the Diablo Mountains to the valley of San Joaquin by the Pacheco Pass, thence down the valley until about opposite the mouth of the Merced River, thence across the San Joaquin, and up into the Sierra Nevada, to the mammoth trees of Mariposa and the glorious Yo Semite valley, thence down the Merced to this place. No matter what direction I traveled, I waded in flowers by day and slept with them by night. Hundreds of flowery gems, of most surpassing loveliness, touched my feet and buried them out of sight at every step. I was very happy, the larks and insects sang in streams of unmeasured joy, a sky of plants beneath me, and a sky of light above me, all kept by their Maker in perfect beauty and pure as heaven.[5]

John Muir, photo by Carlton E. Watkins, San Francisco, circa 1875. John Muir Papers, Holt-Atherton Library Special Collections, UOP. Copyright 1984 Muir-Hanna Trust.

When I first set out [September 1867], on the long excursion that finally led me to California, I wandered afoot and alone, from Indiana to the Gulf of Mexico, with a plant-press on my back, holding a generally southward course, like the birds when they are going from summer to winter. From the west coast of Florida I crossed the gulf to Cuba and enjoyed the rich tropical flora there for four happy weeks in January and February. I was intending to go thence to South America, get ashore anywhere on the north end of the continent, make my way through the woods to the headwaters of the Amazon, and float down that grand river to the ocean. But I was unable to find a ship bound for South America — fortunately perhaps, for I had incredibly little money for so long a trip, less than a hundred dollars, and had not yet fully recovered from a fever caught in the Florida swamps. Therefore I decided to postpone my South American trip and visit California for a year or two to see its wonderful flora and the famous Yosemite Valley, the big trees and the vegetation in general. All the world was before me and every day was a holiday, so it did not seem important which one of the world's wildernesses I first should wander into.[6]

My health, which suffered such wreck in the South, has been thoroughly patched and mended in the mountains of California. I came to life in the cool winds and crystal waters of the mountains. A month in the Sierras has effected a complete cure, and I am well again. Were it not for a thought, now and then, of loneliness and isolation, the pleasure of my existence would be complete. I have not received a single letter from anyone since my departure from Florida, and of course I am very lonesome and hunger terribly for the communion of friends. But I mean to settle here eight or nine months, and hope to see this big gap in tidings from friends well mended.[7]

This is a splendid country, and one might truthfully make use of more than half of the Methodist hymn 'Land of pure delight' in describing it: it flows with more of milk and more of honey than ever did old Canaan in its happiest prime. Of all the bright shining ranks of happy days that God has given me since I left Wisconsin, these of California are the happiest.[8]

New York to California

I sailed to New York on a schooner loaded with oranges. On our arrival the captain, knowing something of the lightness of my purse, told me that I could continue to occupy my bed on the ship until I sailed for California, getting my meals at a nearby restaurant. "This is the way we are all doing," he said. Consulting the newspapers, I found that the first ship sailed for Aspinwall in about ten days, and that the steerage passage to San Francisco by way of the Isthmus was only forty dollars,[9] and I started for California weeds and trees the next Thursday on the steamship Santiago de Cuba.[10, 11]

The day before the sailing of the Panama ship [March 13, 1868] I bought a pocket map of California[12] and allowed myself to be persuaded to buy a dozen large maps, mounted on rollers, with a map of the world on one side and the United States on the other. In vain I said I had no use for them. "But surely you want to make money in California, don't you? Everything out there is very dear. We'll sell you a dozen of these fine maps for two dollars each and you can easily sell them in California for ten dollars apiece." I foolishly allowed myself to be persuaded. The maps made a very large, awkward bundle, but fortunately it was the only baggage I had except my little plant press and a small India rubber bag.[13] I laid them in my berth in the steerage, for they were too large to be stolen and concealed.[14]

The scenery of the ocean was intensely interesting, very far exceeding in beauty and magnificence the highest of my most ardent conceptions. There was a savage contrast between life in the steerage and my fine home on the little ship fruiter. Never before had I seen such a barbarous mob, especially at meals.[15]

When the ship arrived at Aspinwall-Colon, I had half a day to ramble about and collect specimens before starting across the Isthmus. I saw only a very little of the tropical grandeur of Panama, for my health was still in wreck, and I did not venture to wait for the arrival of another steamer. The isthmus train moved at cruel speed through the gorgeous Eden of vines and palms, and I could only gaze from the car platform, and weep and pray that the Lord would some day give me strength to see it better.[16]

San Francisco

After a delightful sail among the scenery of the sea we reached San Francisco about the first of April. I only stayed in San Francisco one day and then enquired of a man who was carrying carpenter's tools the nearest way out of town, to get to the uncultivated wild part of the state. He in wonder asked "But where do you want to go?" and I said "anywhere that is wild." This reply startled him. He seemed to fear I might be crazy and therefore the sooner I was out of town the better, so he directed me to the Oakland ferry and told me to cross the Bay there, and said that that would be as good a way out of town as any.[17]

On the second day of April, 1868, I left San Francisco for Yosemite Valley, companioned by a young Englishman. The orthodox route of "nearest and quickest" was by steam to Stockton, thence by stage to Coulterville or Mariposa, and the remainder of the way over the mountains on horseback. But we had plenty of time, and proposed drifting leisurely mountainward, via the valley of San Jose, Pacheco Pass, and the plain of San Joaquin, and thence to Yosemite by any road that we chanced to find; enjoying the flowers and light, "camping out" in our blankets wherever overtaken by night, and paying very little compliance to roads or times. Accordingly, we crossed "the Bay" by

East Oakland, 1868 Photo courtesy of Oakland Public Library

the Oakland ferry, and leaving the train at East Oakland we took the first road we came to and proceeded up the valley of San Jose. The Oakland hills at this time, after a very rainy season,[18] were covered with flowers—patches of yellow and blue and white in endless variety —that made the slopes of the hills seem like a brilliant piece of patch-work.[19]

Santa Clara Valley

We proceeded up the Santa Clara Valley to San Jose. It was the bloom-time of the year. The landscapes were fairly drenched with sunshine, all the air was quivering with the songs of the meadow-larks, and the hills were so covered with flowers that they seemed to be painted. Slow indeed was my progress through these glorious gardens, the first of the California flora I had seen. Cattle and cultivation were making few scars as yet, and I wandered enchanted in long wavering curves, knowing by my pocket map that Yosemite Valley lay to the east and that I should surely find it.[20]

The valley of San Jose is one of the most fertile of the many small valleys of the coast ranges; its rich bottoms are filled with wheat fields and orchards and vineyards, and alfalfa meadows. It was now spring-time, and the weather was the best that we ever enjoyed. Larks and streams sang everywhere; the sky was cloudless, and the whole valley was a lake of light.[21]

The atmosphere was spicy and exhilarating; my companion acknowledging over his national prejudices, that it was the best he ever breathed; more deliciously fragrant than the hawthorn hedges of England. This San Jose sky was not simply pure and bright, and mixed with plenty of well tempered sunshine, but it possessed a positive flavor, — a taste that thrilled, from the lungs throughout every tissue of the body; every inspiration yielded a corresponding well-defined piece of pleasure that awakened thousands of new palates everywhere. Both my companion and myself had lived and dozed on common air for nearly thirty years, and never before this had discovered that our bodies contained such multitudes of palates or that this mortal flesh, so little valued by philosophers and teachers, was possessed of so vast a capacity for happiness.[22]

Downtown San Jose looking southeast towards the Diablo range, 1868
Sourisseau Academy, San Jose State University

We emerged from this ether baptism new creatures, born again; and truly not until this time were we fairly conscious that we were born at all. Never more, I thought, as we strode forward at faster speed, never more shall I sentimentalize about getting out of the mortal coil: this flesh is not a coil, its a sponge steeped in immortality.[23]

The last of the Coast Range foothills were in near view all the way to Gilroy; those of the Monte Diablo range on our left, those of Santa Cruz on our right. They were smooth and flowing, and their union with the valley was by curves and courses of most surpassing beauty. They were robed with the greenest grass and richest light I ever beheld, and were colored and shaded with myriads of flowers of every hue, which did not occur singly or in handfuls, scattered about in the grass, but grew close together, in smooth cloud-shaped companies, acres and hill-sides in size, white, purple, and yellow, separate, yet blending to each other like the hills upon which they grew. Besides the white, purple, and yellow clouds, we occasionally saw a thicket of scarlet castilleias and silvery-leaved lupines, also splendid fields of wild oats (Avena fatua). The delightful gilia (G. tricolor) was very abundant in sweeping hillside sheets, and a Leptosiphon

(L. androsca) and Claytonias were everywhere by the roadsides, and lilies and dodecatheons by the streams: no wonder the air was so good, waving and rubbing on such a firmament of flowers![24]

Hundreds of crystal rills joined song with the larks, filling all the valley with music like a sea, making it Eden from end to end. I tried to decide which of the plant-clouds was most fragrant: perhaps it was the white, composed mostly of a delicate Boragewort; but doubtless all had a hand in balming the sky. Among trees we observed were the laurel (Oreodaphne californica), and magnificent groves and tree-shaped groups of oaks, some specimens over seven feet in diameter; the white oaks (Quercus lobata) and (Q. douglasii), the black oak (Q. sonomensis), live oak (Q. agrifolia), together with several dwarfy species on the hills whose names we did not know. The prevailing north-west wind has permanently swayed all unsheltered trees up the valley; groves upon the more exposed hillsides lean forward like patches of lodged wheat. The Santa Cruz Mountains have grand forests of redwood (Sequoia sempervirens), some specimens near fifty feet in circumference.[25]

Pacheco Pass

Passing through San Jose and going on to Gilroy, I began to enquire the way to Yosemite and they said you had to cross the Coast Range through the Pacheco Pass, go over to the San Joaquin, and then enquire the way there. The goodness of the weather as we journeyed toward Pacheco was beyond all praise and description — fragrant, mellow, and bright. The sky was perfectly delicious, sweet enough for the breath of angels; every draught of it gave a separate and distinct piece of pleasure. I do not believe that Adam and Eve ever tasted better in their balmiest nook.[26]

The Pacheco Pass was scarcely less enchanting than the valley. It resounded with crystal waters, and the loud shouts of thousands of California quails. In size these about equal the eastern quail; not quite so plump in form. The male has a tall, slender crest, wider at top than bottom, which he can hold straight up, or droop backward on his neck, or forward over his bill, at pleasure; and, instead of "Bob White",

Picnic in Coyote Valley, circa 1880,
Sourisseau Academy, San Jose State University

he shouts: "pe-check-a," bearing down with a stiff, obstinate emphasis on "check."[27]

Through a considerable portion of the pass the road bends and mazes along the groves of a stream, or down in its pebbly bed, leading one, now deep in the shadows of dogwoods and alders, then out in the light, through dry chaparral, over green carex meadows banked with violets and ferns, and dry plantless flood-beds of gravel and sand. The scenery, too, and all of nature in the Pass was fairly enchanting. We found strange and beautiful mountain ferns in abundance all through the pass —some far down in dark canons, as the polypodium and rock-fern, or high on sunlit braes, as Pelloea mucronata. Also we observed the delicate gold-powdered Gynmogramma triangularis, and Peloea andromedoefolia, and the maidenhair (Adiantum chilense), and the broadshouldered bracken (Pteris aquilina), which is everywhere; and an aspidium and cystopteris, and two or three others that I was not acquainted with. Also in this rich garden pass we gathered many fine grasses and carices, and brilliant penstemons, azure and scarlet, and mints and lilies, and scores of others, strangers to us. There were banks of blooming shrubs, and countless assemblies of flowers, beautiful and pure as ever enjoyed the sun or shade of a mountain home.[28]

And oh! What streams were there! Beaming, glancing, each with music of its own, singing as they go, leaping and gliding in shadow and light, onward along their lovely changing pathways to the sea; and hills rise over hills, and mountains rise over mountains, heaving, waving, swelling, in most glorious, overpowering, unreadable majesty.[29]

After we were fairly over the summit of the pass, and had reached an open hill-brow, a scene of peerless grandeur burst suddenly upon us. At our feet, basking in sungold, lay the great Central Plain of California, bounded by the mountains on which we stood, and by the lofty, snowcapped Sierra Nevada; all in grandest simplicity, clear and bright as a new outspread map. Looking down from a height of fifteen hundred feet, extending north and south as far as I could see, lay a vast flower garden, smooth and level like a lake of gold – the floweriest part of the world I had yet seen. From the eastern margin of the golden plain arose the white Sierra; at the base ran a belt of

The Pacheco/Firebaugh Toll Road just west of the pass,
circa 1868, Milliken Museum, Los Banos

gently sloping purplish foothills lightly dotted with oaks, above that a broad dark zone of coniferous forests, and above this forest zone arose the lofty mountain peaks, clad in snow. The atmosphere was so clear that the nearest of the mountain peaks, on the axis of the range, at a distance of more than one hundred and fifty miles, seemed to be at just the right distance to be seen broadly in their relations to one another, marshaled in glorious ranks and groups. It seemed impossible for a man to walk across the open folds without being seen, even at this distance. Perhaps more than three hundred miles of the range was comprehended in this one view.[30]

The mighty Sierra, miles in height, and so gloriously colored and so radiant, seemed not clothed with light, but wholly composed of it, like the wall of some celestial city. Along the top and extending a good way down, was a rich pearl-gray belt of snow; below it a belt of blue and dark purple, marking the extension of the forests; and stretching along the base of the range a broad belt of rose-purple; all these colors, from the blue sky to the yellow valley, smoothly blending as they do in a rainbow, making a wall of light, ineffably fine. Then it seemed to me that the Sierra should be called, not the Nevada or Snowy Range, but the Range of Light.[31]

Boat on San Joaquin River at Hill's Ferry, 1865

San Joaquin Valley

In half a day we were down over all the foothills, past the San Luis Gonzaga Ranch, and wading out in the grand level ocean of flowers. This plain, watered by the San Joaquin and Sacramento rivers, formed one flowerbed nearly four hundred miles in length by thirty in width — a smooth sea, ruffled a little in the middle by the trees fringing the river, and here and there by smaller cross streams from the mountains. One can scarce believe that these vast assemblies of flower families are permanent, but rather that actuated by some great special plant purpose, they have convened from every plain and mountain and meadow of their kingdom, and that each different coloring marked the boundaries of the various tribe and family encampments.[32]

Florida is indeed a land of flowers, but for every single flower-creature that dwells in that most delightsome place, more than a hundred are living here. Here, here is Florida![33] Here flowers are not sprinkled apart with grass between as on our prairies, but grasses are sprinkled among the flowers; not as in Cuba, flowers piled upon flowers, heaped and gathered into deep glowing masses, but flowers side by side, raceme to raceme, petal to petal, touching but not entwined, branches weaving past and past each other but free and separate — one level sheet. True, in looking at this flower robe more closely it would seem to be thrice folded, mosses next to the ground, petaled flowers above them, grasses over all; but to our eyes they are one.[34]

Crossing this greatest of flower gardens, and then the San Joaquin River at Hill's Ferry, I drifted separate for many days in this botanist's better land, the largest days of my life, resting at times from the blessed plants in showers of bugs and sun-born butterflies; or I watched the smooth-bounding antelopes, or startled hares, skimming light and swift as eagles' shadows; or turning from all this fervid life, contemplating the Sierra, that mighty wall uprising from the brink of this lake of gold, miles in the higher blue, bearing aloft its domes and spires in spotless white, unshining and beamless, yet pure as pearl, clear and undimmed as the flowers at my feet. Never were mortal eyes more thronged with beauty.[35]

23

The yellow of the Compositae is pure, deep, bossy solar gold, as if the sun had filled their rays and flowerets with the undiluted substance of his very self. In depth, the purple stratum was about ten or twelve inches; the yellow, seven or eight, and the moss stratum, of greenish yellow, one inch. But the purple stratum is dilute and transparent, so that the lower yellow is hardly dimmed; and only when a horizontal view is taken, so as to look edgewise through the upper stratum, does its color predominate, Therefore, when one stands on a wide level area, the gold immediately about him seems all in all; but on gradually looking wider the gold dims, and purple predominates. Out of sight is another stratum of purple, the ground forests of mosses, with purple stems, and purple cups. The color-beauty of these mosses, at least in the mass, was not made for human eyes, nor for the wild horses that inhabit these plains, nor the antelopes, but perhaps the little creatures enjoy their own beauty, and perhaps the insects that dwell in these forests and climb their shining columns enjoy it, but we know that however faint, and however shaded, no part of it is lost, for all color is received into the eyes of God.[36]

When I walked, more than a hundred flowers touched my feet, at every step closing above them, as if wading in water. Go where I would, east or west, north or south, I still splashed and rippled in flower-gems; and at night I lay between two skies of silver and gold, spanned by a milkyway of vegetable suns. But all this beauty of life is fading year by year, fading like the glow of a sunset, foundering in the grossness of modern refinement. As larks are gathered in sackfuls, ruffled and blood-stained, to toy morbid appetite in barbarous towns, so is flower-gold gathered to slaughter pens in misbegotten carcasses of oxen and sheep. So always perish the plant peoples of temperate regions, — feeble, unarmed, unconfederate, they are easily overthrown, leaving their lands to man and his few enslavable beasts and grasses. But vigorous flower nations of the South, armed and combined, hold plantfully their rightful kingdom; and woe to the lordly biped trespassing in these tropic gardens; catbriers seam his flesh, and saw-palmettoes grate his bones, and bayonets glide to his joints and marrow. But, alas! only one plant of this plain is armed; a tall purple mint, speared and lanced like a thistle. The weapons of plants are believed by some to be a consequence of "man's first disobedience". Would that all the flowers of the Sacramento and San Joaquin, were "cursed", thorned and thistled in safety![37]

Botanical Information

In order that some definite conception may be formed of the richness of this flower-field, I will give a harvest gathered by me from one square yard of plain, opposite Hill's Ferry, a few miles from the coast range foothills, and taken at random, like a cupful of water from a lake. An approximation was made to the number of grass flowers by counting the panicles, to the flowers of the Compositae by counting the heads. The mosses were roughly estimated by counting the number growing on one square inch. All the flowers of the other natural orders were counted one by one.

Natural Orders	no. of flowers	no. of species.
Graminaceae -	29,830	3 (1,000 panicles, 700 stems)
Compositae -	132, 125	2 yellow (3,305 heads)
Legunimosae -	2,620	2 purple and white
Umbelliferae -	620	1 yellow
Polemoniaceae -	401	2 purple
Scrophulariaceae -	169	1 purple
Rubiaceae -	40	1 white
Geraniaceae -	22	1 purple

Natural order unknown - 85   1

Natural order unknown - 60 (plants unflowered, yellow)

Musci [mosses]- 1,000,000 – 2 purple (Funaria and Dicranum)

Total number of natural orders- 9 to 11.

Total number of species- 16 - 17.

Total number of open flowers- 165, 912.

Total number of mosses- 1,000,000.

In the above estimate, only open living flowers were taken into account. Those which were still in bud, together with those that were past flower, would number nearly as many more. The heads of

Post Office in early spring, Snelling, circa 1870, Merced County Historical Society

the Compositae are usually regarded as one flower. Even then we would have seven thousand two hundred and sixty-two flowers, together with a thousand silky, transparent panicles of grasses, and a floor an inch thick of hooded mosses. The grasses have scarce any eaves, and do not interfere with the light of the other flowers, or with their color, in any marked degree.[38]

February and March are the ripe springtime of the plain, April the summer, and May the autumn. The first beginnings of spring are controlled by the rains, which generally appear in December. Rains between May and December are very rare. This is the winter, a winter of drought and heat. But in no part of the year is plant-life wholly awanting. A few lilies with bulbs very deep in the soil, and a rosy compound called tarweed, and a species of erigonum, are slender, inconspicuous links, which continue the floral chain from season to season, around the year.[39]

Foothills

I had a week or two of fever before leaving the plains for Yo Semite, but it was not severe, I was only laid up three or four days, and ere we were ready to recommence our march to Yosemite, May was about half done. On this part of my journey I was joined by a young Englishman by the name of Chilwell,[40] a most amusing companion, and we had several accidents and adventures. We followed the Merced River, which I knew drained Yosemite Valley, and ascended the foothills from Snelling by way of Coulterville.[41]

The flowers and grasses, so late in the pomp and power of full bloom, were dead, and their parched leaves crisped and crackled beneath our feet, as if they had literally been "cast into the oven." They were not given weeks and months to grow old; but they aged and died ere they could fade, standing side by side, erect and undecayed, bearing seed-cells and urns beautiful as corollas. After riding for two days in this autumn, we found summer again in the higher Sierra foothills. Flowers were spread confidingly open, the grasses waved their branches all bright and gay in the colors of healthy prime, and the winds and streams were cool. Above Coulterville, forty or fifty miles farther in the mountains, we came to spring. The leaves of the mountain-oaks were small and drooping, and still wore their first tintings of crimson and purple; and the wrinkles of their bud-folds were still distinct, as if newly opened; and, scattered over banks and sunny, mild sloping places, thousands of gentle mountain flowers were tasting life for the first time.[42]

At the little mining town of Coulterville we bought flour and tea and made inquiries about roads and trails, and the forests we would have to pass through. The storekeeper, an Italian, took kindly pains to tell the pair of wandering wayfarers, new arrived in California, that the winter had been very severe, that in some places the Yosemite trail was still buried in snow eight or ten feet deep, and therefore we would have to wait at least a month before we could possibly get into the great valley, for we would surely get lost should we attempt to go on. As to the forests, the trees, he said, were very large; some of the pines eight or ten feet in diameter.[43]

In reply I told him that it would be delightful to see snow ten feet deep and trees ten feet thick, even if lost, but I never got lost in wild woods. "Well," said he, "go, if you must, but I have warned you;

27

and anyhow you must have a gun, for there are bears in the mountains, but you must not shoot at them unless they come for you and are very, very close up." So at last, at Mr. Chilwell's anxious suggestion, we bought an old army musket with a few pounds of quail shot and large buckshot, good, as the merchant assured us, for either birds or bears.[44]

Our bill of fare in our camps was simple: tea and cakes, the latter toasted on the coals, made from flour without any leaven. Chilwell, being an Englishman, loudly lamented being compelled to live on flour and water, as he expressed it, and hungered for flesh. Therefore he made desperate efforts to shoot something to eat: quail and grouse, etc., but he was invariably unsuccessful, a poor shot, and declared the gun was of no use. I told him I thought that it was a good gun, if properly loaded and properly aimed, and that at the first camp we made I would show him how to load the gun and how to shoot.[45]

At a height of one thousand feet or so we found many of the lily family blooming in all their glory, the Calochortus especially, a charming genus like European tulips, but finer, and many species of two new shrubs—especially, Ceanothus and Adenostoma. The oaks, beautiful trees with blue foliage and white bark, forming open groves, gave a fine

Coulterville, before the fire of 1879. The gold boom increased the population to around 10,000 people.

125th Commemorative Issue - Mariposa Gazette 1854 - 1979 Page 108

Coulterville Before the Fire of 1879, Mariposa Museum and History Center

park-like effect. Higher, we met the first of the pines, with long gray foliage, large stout cones, and wide-spreading heads like palms. Then yellow pines, growing gradually more abundant as we ascended.[46]

At Bower Cave, on the north fork of the Merced River, the streams were fringed with willows and azalea, ferns, flowering dogwood, etc. Here, too, we enjoyed the strange beauty of the Cave in a limestone hill. At Deer Flat the wagon road ended in a trail, which we traced up the side of the dividing ridge parallel to the Merced and Tuolumne. A few miles farther "onward and upward", on the Pilot Peak ridge, we came again to the edge of winter. Scarce a grass or growing leaf was to be seen. The last of the lilies and spring violets were left far below; the winter scales were still wrapt close upon the buds of the dwarf oaks and alders. The great sugar pines waved their long arms solemnly, to the cold, loud, winds among rushing, changing, stormclouds. The sky became darker and more terrible. Many-voiced mountain winds swept the pines, speaking the dread language of the cold north. Snow began to fall thick and blinding, and soon my horse was deep in snow.[47] Thus, in less than a week from the hot autumn of the San Joaquin, we were struggling in a bewildering storm of mountain winter.[48]

Fortunately, we reached Crane Flat, where some mountaineer had tried to establish a claim to the Flat by building a little cabin of sugar pine shakes. Though we had arrived early in the afternoon I decided to camp there for the night, as the trail was buried in the snow that was about six feet deep. I wanted to examine the topography and plan our course. This was on or about May 20, at an elevation of six thousand one hundred and thirty feet. Chilwell cleared away the snow from the door and floor of the cabin, and made a bed of boughs from the fernlike silver fir, though I urged the same sort of bed made under the trees on the snow. But he had the house habit.[49]

Here for the first time I saw the giants of the Sierra woods in all their glory. The forest was magnificent, composed in part of sugar pine (Pinus lambertiana), which is the king of all pines. Many specimens were over two hundred feet in height, eight to ten feet in diameter, fresh and sound as the sun which made them. The yellow pine (Pinus ponderosa) also grew there, and the cedar (Libocedrus decurrens); but the bulk of the forest was made up of the two silver firs (Picea grandis and Picea amabilis), the former always greatly predominating at that altitude. The sugar pine seemed to me the priest of the woods, ever addressing the surrounding trees, and blessing them. I began eagerly to sketch the noblest specimens, trying to draw every leaf and branch.[50]

Chilwell reminded me of my promise about the gun, hoping eagerly for improvement to our bill of fare, however slight. I loaded the gun, paced off thirty yards from the cabin, or shanty, and told Mr. Chilwell to pin a piece of paper on the wall and see if I could not put shot into it and prove the value of the gun. Accordingly Mr. Chilwell pinned on a piece of an envelope on the shanty wall and vanished around the corner of the shanty, calling out "Fire away".[51]

I supposed that he had gone way back of the cabin, but instead he went inside of the cabin and stood up against the mark that he

Bridalveil Fall, Yosemite Valley by Carleton Watkins, circa 1865
from the collection of the Library of Congress

had himself placed on the wall; and as the shake wall was soft sugar pine, only about half an inch thick, the shot passed through it and into his shoulder. He came rushing out, crying in great concern that I had shot him. The weather being cold, he had on three coats and as many shirts, and one of the coats was a heavy English overcoat. I discovered that the shot had passed through all this clothing and the pellets were imbedded beneath the skin and had to be picked out with the point of a pen knife. I said: "Why did you stand against that mark?" He said: "Well, I never thought that the shot would go through the 'ouse."[52]

Leaving Crane Flat, we found our way easily enough over the deep snow, guided by the topography, holding a general easterly direction, getting, now and then, from the top of some headland, a glimpse of the Merced Cañon, which was my main guide. We discovered the trail on the brow of the valley, just as the Bridal Veil came in sight. I didn't know that it was one of the famous falls I had read about, and, calling Chilwell's attention to it I said, "See that dainty little fall over there. I should like to camp at the foot of it to see the ferns and lilies that may be there. It looks small from here, only about fifteen or twenty feet, but it may be sixty or seventy." So little did we then know of Yo Semite magnitudes![53]

Descending these higher mountains towards the Merced, the snow gradually disappeared, tender leaves unfolded less and less doubtfully, violets and lilies appeared about us once more, and at length, arriving in the glorious Yo Semite, we found it full of summer and spring. Thus, as colors blend in a rainbow, and as mountains curve to a plain, so meet and blend the plants and seasons of this delightsome land.[54]

Yosemite

There is a kind of hotel in the valley, but it is incomparably better to choose your own camp among the rocks and waterfalls. And of course we shunned the hotel in the valley, seldom indulging even in crackers, both being too costly. After spending eight or ten days in visiting the falls and the high points of view around the walls, making sketches, collecting flowers and ferns, etc., we decided to make the return trip by the Mariposa trail to see the celebrated grove of Giant Sequoias, by way of Wawona, then owned by Galen Clark, the Yosemite pioneer.[55]

The night before the start was made on the return trip, we camped near the Bridal Veil Meadows, where, as we lay eating our suppers by the light of the campfire, we were visited by a bear. We heard him approaching by the heavy crackling of twigs. Chilwell, in alarm, after listening a while, said, "I see it! I see it! It's a bear, a grizzly! Where is the gun? You take the gun and shoot him — you can shoot best." (I had shot him you remember.) But the gun had only a charge of birdshot in it; therefore, while the bear stood on the opposite side of the fire, at a distance of probably twenty-five or thirty feet, I hastily loaded in a lot of buckshot. The buckshot was too large to chamber and therefore it made a zigzag charge on top of the birdshot charge, the two charges occupying about half of the barrel. Thus armed, the gun held at rest, pointed at the bear, we sat hushed and motionless, according to instructions from the man who sold the gun, solemnly waiting and watching, as full of fear as the musket of shot. Finally, after sniffing and whining for his supper what seemed to us a long time, the young inexperienced beast walked off. We were much afraid of his returning to attack us. We did not then know that bears never attack sleeping campers, and dreading another visit, we kept awake, on guard, most of the night.[56]

Mariposa Grove to Hopeton

Like the Coulterville trail, all the high-lying part of the Mariposa trail was deeply snow-buried, but we found our way, without any tracks to guide us, without the slightest trouble, steering by the topography, in a general way, along the brow of the canyon of the south fork of the Merced River, and in a day or two reached Wawona. Here we replenished our little flour sack and Mr. Clark gave us a piece of bear meat. We then pushed eagerly on up the Wawona ridge through a magnificent sugar pine forest and into the far-famed Mariposa Sequoia Grove. The sun was down when we entered the

Grove, but we soon had a good fire and at supper that night we tasted bear meat for the first time. My flesh-hungry companion ate it eagerly, though to me it seemed so rank and oily that I was unable to swallow a single morsel.[57]

After supper we replenished the fire and gazed enchanted at the vividly illumined brown boles of the giants towering about us, while the stars sparkled in wonderful beauty above their huge domed heads. We camped here long uncounted days, wandering about from tree to tree, taking no note of time. The longer we gazed, the more we admired not only their colossal size, but their majestic beauty and dignity. Greatest of trees, greatest of living things, their noble domes, poised in unchanging repose, seemed to belong to the sky, while the great firs and pines about them looked like mere latter-day saplings, like mere weeds growing among corn, so much was their grandeur dwarfed by these Sequoia Giants.[58]

While we camped in the Mariposa Grove, the abundance of bear tracks caused Mr. Chilwell no little alarm, and he proposed that we load the gun properly with buckshot and without any useless birdshot; but there was no means of drawing the charge. It had to be shot off. The recoil was so great that it bruised his shoulder and sent him spinning like a top. Casting down the miserable gun, kicking the bad luck musket among the Sequoia cones and branches that littered the ground, he stripped and examined his unfortunate shoulder. In painful indignation and wrath, he found it black and blue and more seriously hurt by the bruising recoil blow than by the shot at Crane Flat.[59]

When we got down to the hot San Joaquin plain at Snelling, the grain fields were nearly ready for the reaper, and we began to enquire for a job to replenish our remaining stock of money, which was now very small — though we had not spent much; the grand royal trip of more than a month in the Yosemite region having cost us only about three dollars each.[60, 61]

Looking back on what I have written I see that it is nothing —— just nothing, and it will not carry you a drop, not a drop, my friends, from all these oceans and gulfs and bays of plant loveliness. Can you not come? Just come and see what you can make of these great lessons of mountain and plain. Yo Semite alone is worth the expense and danger of any journey in the world. It is by far the grandest of all of the special temples of Nature I was ever permitted to enter. It must be the *sanctum sanctorum* of the Sierra(s), and I trust that you will all be led to it.[62]

> John Muir
> July, 1868
> Nr. Hopeton

John Muir in Yosemite, circa 1909. John Muir Papers,
Holt-Atherton Library Special Collections, UOP.
Copyright 1984 Muir-Hanna Trust

Part Two:
Creating the Muir Ramble Route

The complete story of Muir's trip gave us all the major land-marks (i.e. Gilroy, Pacheco Pass, etc.) but no specific details. We had to study old maps, some brittle old artifacts in museums, others on microfilm and online, to find his exact route.[1]

John Muir left San Francisco around the first of April in 1868. The trip started in San Francisco at the intersection of Davis and Broadway Streets as that was where the Oakland ferry terminal was located in 1868. Since then the bay has been filled in and today this is a full block from the water's edge. Muir's ferry landed in Oakland, just east of what is today Middle Harbor Shoreline Park. A three-quarter mile long wharf was required to assure service at low tide and a train ran out the wharf, bringing goods and passengers from the ferry into Oakland. The wharf ended near present day Seventh St. and Wood St. There was a West Oakland station near the terminus, and standard service was provided to a station at Seventh St. and Broadway. Muir may have debarked there to walk across the newly built dam on Lake Merritt, at Twelfth St., he may have continued to the next train stop before starting his walk. The next stop was near the intersection of Fourteenth St. and Fourteenth Ave., called "San Antonio" or "Brooklyn". Muir states he left the train in East Oakland so we believe he rode to the second stop and thus the "first road we came to" was modern day East Fourteenth St.

Old maps show that in 1868 there were only two main through-roads between Oakland and San Jose. Both started south on East Fourteenth St. The high road was called the Camino de Rancho San Antonio after the Mexican land grant it ran through. This road followed along the Oakland hills, passing by Mission San Jose. The second road ran along the bay, connecting the farmlands to the shoreline and the landings used for shipping goods. 1867-8 was the San Francisco Bay region's fourth rainiest winter on record so we assume the lower road would have been flooded and muddy. Given this, and the fact that Muir spoke so glowingly of the Oakland hills, we believe Muir took the high road.

Muir followed this "Oakland Road" all the way to San Jose. Even in Muir's day this road had a diversion in Milpitas, circling around land belonging to a farmer who was not willing to give a right of way through his land. Today the road changes names many times on the way, being called International Boulevard through Fruitvale, East Fourteenth in San Leandro, Mission Boulevard in Hayward, North Milpitas Boulevard in Milpitas and the Oakland Road in San Jose.[2]

Muir entered San Jose on Thirteenth St. and left on First St., which becomes the Monterey Rd. He then followed the Monterey Rd., past the still standing 12 and 15 Mile Houses in Coyote, and on to "Old" Gilroy, which was a few miles to the east of the present location. In 1869 the whole town moved to be on the newly constructed railroad line, and today Old Gilroy Rd. can be seen leaving the Monterey Rd. and heading east. From there Muir traveled southeast, skirting the rolling hills of the Diablo Range, following a route used by the Butterfield Stage. This is now called the Pacheco Pass Highway or Highway 152. He passed San Felipe Lake, where early travelers often washed their clothes in the naturally soft water, and continued until he reached the Pacheco Creek. He then followed the creek up to the Pacheco Pass. Today the creek can be found just south of Highway 152. Just past Casa de Fruta there is an old cafe that marks the location of Bell Station, a stage stop in Muir's time.

Muir crossed the Pacheco Pass over the Pacheco Pass Toll Road. The air at the pass was so clear that Muir saw the Sierra and he made his now famous pronouncement that it should not be called Sierra Nevada but rather the "Range of Light." Today Dinosaur Point Road, which leaves Highway 152 just west of the top of the pass, follows the historic route of the Pacheco Pass Toll Road right down to the edge of the San Luis Reservoir. Muir would have continued straight ahead. At that time Rancho San Luis Gonzaga, a cattle ranch and stage stop, was nestled in the center of what was a lush and beautiful valley that is now dammed and flooded.

From San Luis Gonzaga he followed the road to Los Banos, turning north before reaching the San Joaquin River to skirt the east side of the Diablo Range on what 1868 maps label the Whitworth Rd. He then crossed the San Joaquin River just north of the confluence of the Merced and San Joaquin Rivers at Hills Ferry. In Muir's day both rivers were water highways and Hills Ferry was a busy waterfront town. Barges traveled from San Francisco to Fresno on the San Joaquin River and from Hills Ferry to Snelling on the Merced River bringing city goods to the valley farms and valley crops to the city markets. In

Donna and Peter hiking in Henry Coe State Park

1869 the railroad was brought down the west side of the San Joaquin Valley and Hills Ferry was moved a few miles west, building by building, to be situated on the railroad line. The town's name was changed to Newman.

Muir continued east on a road just north of the Merced River, labeled "Road to Hills Ferry" on old Merced County maps. Here Muir "drifted separate for many days in this botanist's better land"[3] and is where he said, "When I walked, more than a hundred flowers touched my feet, at every step closing above them, as if wading in water."[4] He then continued towards the lower foothills, passing through Hopeton and Snelling, both bustling towns in 1868. Snelling was as far as barges could travel on the Merced River and was the county seat. A few years later the honor was given to Merced, a smaller town, but situated on the newly built railroad line. In Snelling locals believe that when Muir was "laid up three or four days"[5] recovering from a bout with malarial fever he stayed in the IOOF (Independent Order of Odd Fellows) building that is still standing on the main street of town.

Muir's initial plan had been to follow the Merced River all the way to the Yosemite Valley. But he changed course after passing through Snelling and left the river to take a route via Coulterville instead. At this time there were no reservoirs and he traveled straight through the land now covered by Don Pedro Lake. He then may have walked up Penon Blanco Rd., as he did the next year when herding the sheep to the Sierra. This road runs just north of present day Highway 132. If so, he followed what is now Highway 49 into Coulterville.

In Coulterville Muir acquired horses, a gun and provisions, then set out following the route to Yosemite first outlined in James Hutchings 1862 book *Scenes of Wonder and Curiosity in California*. This route followed a well-defined wagon road past Bower Cave and Black's Inn to Deer Flat. Today's modern Forest Service road runs north and east of the old road, which stayed closer to Bull Creek. From Deer Flat Muir followed a small horse trail called the Coulterville Free Trail. It took him past Hazel Green and on to Crane Flat. Even though Muir went to Yosemite to see the sequoias he passed right by the Merced Grove, but only because it had not yet been "discovered". That discovery happened a few years later when the Yosemite-Coulterville Road surveyors were trying to find a way to make the little trail into a serviceable road. Muir did see giant sugar pines though. He marveled at their magnificence, calling them "king of all pines". Today there is still a splendid grove of giant sugar pines between Hazel Green and Crane Flat that was saved from the sawmill by the Rockefeller family who bought the grove and surrounding land in the 1930s then donated it to Yosemite National Park. We believe the trees Muir described are in the Rockefeller Grove.

From Crane Flat Muir said "[we]...found our way easily enough over the deep snow, guided by the topography..."[6] He would have been following the route of the Coulterville Free Trail up to Gin Flat and then down to Tamarack Flat. This trail later became the Big Oak Flat Road, which was abandoned in the 1940s because of continual rockslides, and today the old road bed provides a clear trail for the hiker to follow Muir's footsteps.

He found the Free Trail after crossing Cascade Creek and rounding the corner at what would later be known as Gentry's, which served as a toll station for the road completed in 1874 and a sawmill for lumber needed to build lodging in the Yosemite Valley. He gained his first view of Bridalveil Fall and the Yosemite Valley at what is now known both as "Oh My! Point" and "Rainbow View". Muir spent that night camped near the base of Bridalveil Fall and in the following days explored the valley. He then continued on to Clark's Station and the Mariposa Grove of Big Trees, following existing trails that run just east of the modern Highway 41. He then returned to the San Joaquin Valley, where he spent the summer working, traveling by way of Mariposa on what is today called the Chowchilla Mountain Road.

Finding our parallel Muir Ramble Route

Muir was not the only person to follow this route to the Sierra. Since 1849 miners had been crossing the Pacheco Pass to reach Mariposa County's "southern mines", and in 1868 the Butterfield Stage used the Pacheco Pass Toll Road for its overland mail route. But this does not mean Muir knew where he was going. He makes this clear when he stated, "...going on to Gilroy, I began to inquire the way to Yosemite, and there they said, you have to cross the Coast Range and go over to the San Joaquin, and then you have to inquire the way there."[7]

Why did Muir choose to go over the Pacheco Pass, when he knew "the orthodox route of nearest and quickest" was through Stockton? He did not just want to get to Yosemite, he wanted to get out of the civilized places to the places that were wild, "drifting leisurely mountainward, via the valley of San Jose, Pacheco Pass, and the plain of San Joaquin, and thence to Yosemite by any road that we chanced to find; enjoying the flowers and light, "camping out" in our blankets wherever overtaken by night, and paying very little compliance to roads or times..."[8] The answer becomes even more evident after studying Muir's life. At that time his passion was botany. Early guidebooks painted a picture of California being a place of great natural beauty and the Santa Clara Valley as a botanical wonder of the world, a place where plants that could not even grow in a greenhouse back east grew wild in winter.[9] For Muir the choice of route would not have been a question: he would choose the way with the most flowers.

When Donna traced out Muir's route on a modern California map she found that most of the little roads of 1868 were now paved over by busy highways. "But," she pointed out, "All the roads are highways, not freeways, so we can legally walk on them. They may not be picturesque or what Muir would choose to walk, but they will get us to Yosemite." We drove an exploratory trip. It made an interesting road trip but we realized that more than just following Muir's historical footsteps we wanted to capture the spirit of his adventure: to see birds not buildings, rivers not roadways, skylines not shopping malls and wild plants not landscaped medians. We wanted to see the still wild places between San Francisco and Yosemite.

We started buying more maps to explore other options: special trail maps, USGS topographic maps, and National Forest Service maps. A map from the San Francisco Bay Trail Association revealed the existence of a public walking/cycling path along the edge of the bay just a few miles to the west of Muir's actual route. We then noticed similar trail systems running along the Guadalupe River and the Coyote Creek through Santa Clara County. It seemed that with minor detours on city streets we would be able to get all the way from Oakland to Morgan Hill on trails.

In that instant the whole thing fell together. Just as Muir did not follow the expected route to Yosemite we would not follow his exact footsteps. We would walk to Yosemite parallel to Muir's route, not on roads, but on public pathways, bike trails, nature trails, through city, county, state and national parks and open spaces, so that we could experience a natural California. If we had to we would use sidewalks or little streets, or even busy roads, but our goal would be to walk in the spirit of his trip rather than in his exact footsteps, always trying to find the places that still looked and felt like the California Muir experienced in 1868. We would make it a walk through history, reading other travel accounts from California in the late 1800s to better understand what Muir would have seen and experienced. It would be a "scouting party" to find an urban hiking route that would give nature-loving Bay Area residents a way to walk where they usually drive in cars. We were so excited we could already imagine a future with little hostels and cafes springing up along our new route to house and feed travelers on the trek to Yosemite.

Our first trip on the Muir Ramble Route

We took our first walking trip to Yosemite in 2006. We called it the "Trans-California Ramble" because like Muir, we planned to take time to notice our surroundings and enjoy nature. To honor Muir and create a public awareness of the need for a trans-California public walking route we set up presentations at public libraries and local history societies along the way. We also created a web site about the project and posted daily accounts of what we saw and experienced as we walked (www.johnmuir.org/walk).

We left San Francisco on April 2, 2006, the same day Muir left, but 138 years later. We then spent the next month walking to Yosemite following the 300-mile "Muir Ramble Route" we had mapped out. Just like Muir, we began our trip by taking the ferry to Oakland. We then followed the Bay Trail's intermittent bike paths through Alameda County, then passed through the Santa Clara Valley following the Coyote Creek and Guadalupe River corridors. We backpacked over the Diablo Range on hiking trails through Henry Coe State Park, crossed the San Joaquin Valley beside irrigation ditches and climbed the Sierra Nevada foothills on a combination of small rural roads and busy highways. From Coulterville we backpacked on dirt and gravel roads through National Forest land, and finally descended into the Yosemite Valley via Crane Flat and Tamarack Flat on wilderness hiking trails.

The trip was about 300 miles and took about 30 days. As we walked we experienced anew places that had once been only colorful blurs from a car window as we drove past at sixty-five miles per hour. We fell in love with California's natural beauty and diverse landscapes. We began to understand the relationship between the various mountain ranges, river valleys and watersheds. We looked with John Muir's eyes and saw the changes in weather and light. We felt his ecstasy as we passed hillsides riotously colored with blooming wildflowers. Each weathered barn and each crumbling dry stone wall told us a story. It was glorious and life changing. I became a confirmed long distance walker, reveling in the outdoor life and my new ability to walk so far in a day. Seeing the light change during the day, the weather change over the month, the seasons make their slow but perceptible changes, I became more attuned to the world around me, and in some unexplainable way, more at peace with the world inside me.

Urban backpacking

If wilderness backpacking is traveling through the wilderness, carrying all you need on your back, sleeping where you end the day's hike and beginning from the same place when you wake up, then what we did should be called "urban backpacking". As urban backpackers we followed routes that wove through cities and rural areas, along river corridors, bike trails, even roads when necessary, to find havens of wilderness where the beauty of nature is still evident. It has been suggested it might be better to call what we did "guerilla backpacking", because of the difficulty involved in trying to travel on foot across the modern highway-dominated landscape; but "guerilla" often implies something outside the law and there is nothing illegal about following the route we outline in the MRR directions. We think of it as an exciting and new way to take an adventure.

Creating the guidebook

Donna and I came home from our Trans-California Ramble with the dream of the route becoming a destination walking trail, like the John Muir Trail in California's Sierra or Spain's Camino de Santiago de Compostela. To this end we started writing this guide book, but immediately found problems that needed to be resolved before the route would be ready for others to follow. First off, we had walked through private land on the east side of the Diablo Range and needed to find a safe and legal route that anyone could use to cross the Pacheco Pass. We had to find legal places to spend each night. Finally, not everyone was going to be able to take 30 days to travel the whole route in a single trip.

As we returned to our maps, we remembered the suggestion ecologist John Olmsted had made when walking with us on the Trans-California Ramble: "Make the trip multi-modal; hike some places, bike others, use public transportation and as a last recourse, where there is no other option, drive." Like in the cartoons, lights went on in our heads: we would divide the trip into logical geographical sections, each would have a separate trip that could be completed in a few days or over a long weekend. Where we had problems finding lodging spaced a day's hike apart we could recommend cycling. Where there were only highways connecting the sections, as up the Pacheco Pass on Highway 156, we could recommend using an automobile shuttle to connect them.

We have now hiked the whole trip continuously once, and have traveled every section at least three times. We have ridden on bikes, we have traveled with other couples and larger groups. The MRR is a wonderful route to follow whatever way you do it. Don't just take our word for it, ask others who have already tried following the MRR: In 2008 we backpacked the MRR from Oakland to Morgan Hill a with group of students from De Anza College engaged in a project to document the migration corridors available to animals in the South Santa Clara Valley. One student wrote, "I knew I was in shape – I played football all through high school, but I wondered if I could do it. And I did, I walked from Oakland to Morgan Hill. I am outside a lot, but on this trip my eyes were opened. I had never noticed all the kinds of trees or thought to look for birds or insects. When you go to a place like Yosemite you *expect* beauty, but not in a place like Fremont. I have a whole bunch of family that lives in Fremont and they don't have a clue about all the natural beauty that is so close by. And if they don't get out there to see it they will never know what they are missing."

"I loved reading what John Muir wrote about a place then seeing it myself. In the beginning we were walking on the shoreline. We could see the Coyote Hills from the trail, but they looked so tiny. I remember I thought, 'Are you kidding me? I can't believe that we're going to go there today.' At the same time I could see Oakland from the same place. It looked so tiny too. It was so incredible, the place where we started walking from and where we were going both looked so tiny. It is so cool that this trail exists plugged right in the city. There are people all around us, hustling and bustling around in their cars going from here to there, and we are walking along by the bay, drifting leisurely from Oakland to Morgan Hill."

With De Anza College students on the Bay Trail

Part Three:
Guidebook to the Muir Ramble Route

This chapter provides the information and directions for following the 305 mile Muir Ramble Route from San Francisco to Yosemite. The MRR is divided into seven sections. Each section contains both directions for through hiking and a recommended trip that can be completed over a long weekend. For easy reference the directions are designated by miles from San Francisco.

Each of the seven sections begins with a summary of the route. This is followed by a description of the Recommended Trip and alternate or side trips. Next is a list of specific things you will need or need to know, like maps and accommodations. Following that is trailhead access information. Finally, there are directions for following the route. We will maintain a website to post trail updates and further information about using the MRR. (www.johnmuir.org/walk/)

The Muir Ramble Route is varied and challenging and wonderful, an ideal urban hiking vacation for residents of the San Francisco Bay Area. Some sections of the trip are so rural that it is easy to imagine it is still 1868 and John Muir is walking right beside you. Other places are so urban that you might find yourself wishing you were back in 1868 on a little dirt road beside John Muir. The MRR is urban backpacking at its finest. Not only does it offer the opportunity to experience first hand the breathtaking changes found in California's landscape it is a sort of journey through the history of California with Muir as your guide.

Section One: San Francisco Bay Area

This section crosses the Bay, rambles along the intermittent San Francisco Bay Trail, and then follows river corridor trails from Milpitas to Morgan Hill. The Recommended Trip can be done either as a two to three day bike trip, or a five to six day walk, and it encompasses the whole section. In both cases there are hotels to stay in every night, and there is one campground directly on the route.

Section Two: Diablo Range

This section climbs through the wilderness of Henry Coe State Park following the Diablo Range south to Highway 152 near Pacheco Pass. The Recommended Trip is a 3-5 day wilderness backpacking trip that encompasses the entire section. Mountain bikes are allowed in the park, however we recommend walking to see all the wonderful native wildflowers that can make the trip so amazing to someone trying on their "John Muir eyes". Camping is allowed throughout the park.

Section Three: Pacheco Pass

This section crosses the Pacheco Pass then descends through wildlife areas managed by the California Department of Fish and Game into the San Joaquin Valley. The Recommended Trip is a long one-day trip that requires walking along a mile of busy highway. We offer two loop trips from the pass as another way to enjoy this section of the MRR. There are campgrounds at both trailheads.

Section Four: San Joaquin Valley

This section crosses the farmlands of the San Joaquin Valley from the O'Neill Forebay, just west of Highway 5, to Ballico, which is just east of Highway 99. The Recommended Trip, which encompasses the whole section, is a two or three day bike trip that follows irrigation canals and picturesque little roads. There are campgrounds to stay in every night. There is also a recommended side trip following Muir's paddle strokes - a float down the Merced River.

Section Five: The Lower Foothills

This section traverses the lower foothills, as they gently rise towards the Sierra, from Ballico to Coulterville. The entire route makes a nice two-day trip for the confident street cyclist, with campgrounds at the beginning, end and half-way point. There are no daily lodging options for the hiker. The Recommended

Trip is an 11-mile day hike on a rural ranch road that passes just east of the place Muir called Twenty Hill Hollow.

Section Six: The Upper Foothills

This section ascends the upper foothills from Coulterville to Yosemite National Park. The Recommended Trip follows small county roads and unpaved National Forest Service roads through the oaks and pines of the Stanislaus National Forest. It is 35 miles, encompasses the entire section, and can be done either as a three-day backpack or a two-day mountain bike ride. There are un-improved campgrounds to stay in each night.

Section Seven: Yosemite

This section wanders along unimproved and little known trails through the wilds of Yosemite National Park. It begins at the Merced Grove trailhead on Highway 120 and ends at the Le Conte Memorial Lodge in Yosemite Valley. The Recommended Trip is a two-day wilderness backpack trip that encompasses the entire section. There is camping half way at the Tamarack Flat Campground and near the ending trailhead.

General things you will need or need to know

When to take the trip

Take your trip following the MRR in the spring: it will be too hot in the summer, too wet in the winter, and in the fall it will be hard to find water in some places. Spring is when the wildflowers are blooming, the temperatures are comfortable and the waterfalls in Yosemite are the most glorious. We suggest hik-ing through Henry Coe Park and the Pacheco Pass area at the height of the wildflower season, camping in the San Joaquin before the mosquitoes hatch, and walking from Crane Flat into Yosemite after the snow begins to melt, but before the Tioga Road opens.

California spring weather varies from day to day and year to year. This must be taken into account when planning your trip. It was only by chance that Muir saw all the wildflowers. If he had arrived a month earlier or later, or the winter had been drier, he may have missed the flower bloom. Some years the rains linger into late April, while in others there is still snow near Crane Flat as late as the end of June. Generally a good time to begin is mid-April, just a bit later than Muir's departure date of April 2nd.

Walk or cycle?

If John Muir walked, why do we sometimes recommend cycling? Although it is true that Muir walked most of the way, he also took a ferry, a train and rode a horse, and we think he would probably approve of cycling the MRR in his honor. It is a little publicized fact, but Muir was a cyclist. We don't know how avid his passion was, but he did take at least one long trip on a bike: In 1915, Stanford professor Melville Anderson wrote that he and Muir had "propelled our bicycles the ninety odd miles from Stanford University to the Alhambra Valley..."[1]

Today most cities and unincorporated county areas have laws that make it illegal to spend the night sleeping outdoors. We can no longer just camp out as Muir did, "in our blankets wherever overtaken by night." And so there are places on the MRR where there are not options for legal lodging spaced an average day's hike, or 10 – 20 miles, apart. Until this situation changes, combining use of a bicycle, or public transportation, with walking makes a trip on the MRR legally possible.

Cycling and walking are both self-powered, and therefore both environmentally friendly forms of transportation, but they are very different experiences. The average speed when walking is about 2-3 mph, while the average speed on a bicycle is about 8-12 mph. On a bike you will be able to cover many more miles, see much more of the California landscape in a single day than on foot. You will be able to entertain the thought of going to a campground or restaurant that is too far off the route to consider when on foot. When walking, there is time to "botanize", time to experience the places you pass through, time to observe small details like the beauty of a lupine flower or follow the slimy path of a multi-colored snail crossing the trail. Both modes have their advantages and disadvantages.

Shuttling

It is difficult to follow the MRR without being driven to some of the trailheads. This will change with improvements in public transportation and acquisition of right-of-ways. In some cases driving two cars is the easiest way to shuttle between trailheads. Traveling with a group of friends and one shuttle vehicle would be an even greener approach. The driver, perhaps someone who loves adventure and the outdoors but is not able to walk or cycle, may choose to join the group for part of the day but must return to the shuttle vehicle in time to get to the trail's end and secure lodging, buy food, etc. for the rest of the group. Alternatively the driver might spend the day visiting local historical sites, or studying some aspect of the regional ecology, then, as after-dinner entertainment share what they learned. If you only have a four-passenger car, but have 5 or more people, we suggest you rent a passenger van with racks, or a trailer, for the bikes. Our experience is that the pleasure of having only one shuttle vehicle to drive will make it worth the extra expense.

Public transportation

Some sections of the MRR have public transportation (bus, train or taxi) options available to access the trailheads. Use these and you won't have to backtrack to get your car or worry about where to leave it. Your trip will be greener, and our experience has been that it will also be more fun. It takes planning and time to use public transportation but there can be great satisfaction in carefully cobbling together routes and schedules and thus avoid using a car!

Clothes and equipment for walking

Traveling through the wilderness is different than traveling through urban areas. In the wilderness you will need all of the standard backpacking gear, but in urban areas there is no reason to be burdened with stuff like a stove, cooking pot and water filter when you are walking where you won't need it.

Clothes: Pack light. Bring clothes that layer or do two jobs. For example bring lightweight synthetic zip off pants instead of heavy cotton jeans and shorts. We have found that our standard

Hiking in Henry Coe State Park

backpacking clothes work perfectly on this trip. Here is what we carried, from top to bottom: sun hat, wool stocking cap, bandanna (doubles as a towel), waterproof windbreaker, down vest, long sleeve button-down shirt, long-sleeved fleece pullover, micro fiber tee shirt, zip-off pants, two pairs of underwear, two pairs of socks, super-lightweight shoes for evenings and shoes or boots for the road. Optional clothes: rain pants, a clean shirt for evening wear and silk long underwear to sleep in.

Footwear

We assumed that since we were hiking we should wear hiking boots, but the soles were too hard for pavement walking and the bottoms of our feet started to bruise after about ten miles. We learned to wear footwear appropriate for the section: hiking boots or trail-runners in the backcountry, cushioned walking or running shoes on the streets.

Equipment

Bring the lightest equipment you can afford. Try to carry no more than 25 pounds without food. Our equipment list includes: a 3.5-pound two-person tent, lightweight sleeping bag (under 2 pounds – if it gets cold just wear all your clothes), lightweight inflatable sleeping pad, backpacking stove, titanium pot, spoon, pocketknife, lightweight bowl (with screw on top for holding leftovers), cup, water filter (purify all water from lakes and streams), first aid kit, toothbrush and sunscreen and other toiletries. We do allow ourselves a few extras. Donna carries her watercolor paints, paper and plant identification books. I carry my ukulele and a harmonica, which I play while Donna paints.

A few useful tips: We carry a short section of foam pad to sit on during the day and add under our pads at night. We use a super lightweight daypack for one of our stuff sacks, and then have a spare pack when we need it. Our cup has a screw-on lid so it can be used for rehydrating a dried dinner during the days' hike, or used as a leftover container.

Note: Make sure your water filter or water purifying tablets are rated to deal with Giardia lamblia and cryptosporidium.

Clothes and equipment for cycling

Clothes: The same clothes suggested for backpacking will also work for cycling. You will need to add three things: gloves, padded bike shorts and a helmet. If you are not a regular cyclist you may not be used to wearing the padded shorts, but they are essential to cushion you on long rides. The cycling gloves will help you avoid blisters and the helmet may save your life!

Equipment: Ride a mountain or hybrid bike. Some of the MRR trail surfaces are dirt or sand, with rocks and potholes, and you will need fatter tires than are on a regular street bike. Bring a tire patch kit, pump, bike light and bike lock. You may enjoy the ease of riding an electric bike as Donna did on our 2007 trip. She had no problem finding places to recharge the battery.

Maps

Carry maps with you at all times. You will need them for general reference and especially if you have to take a detour. We recommend what maps will be needed and where you can find them at the beginning of each section.

Water and restrooms

There are drinking fountains and restrooms along the MRR, but they are erratically spaced and not always working or open. This is a thing that we hope to see change in the future. Carry drinking water with you at all times.

Accommodations

Hotels, campgrounds, private homes, community centers and churches can all provide housing for the wandering MRR traveler. Staying in hotels may be a little more expensive, but you can carry a lighter pack as you will not need much camping gear. Plan your lodging at or near the end of each day's ramble so that you can start the next day from the same place with little effort. We found shuttling from trail to lodging and back tedious, the most time consuming and anticlimactic part of the trip. When we have eliminated shuttling we have always enjoyed ourselves more. The little string of hostels we envision for the future does not yet exist, but when it does everyone will be happier.

MRR Etiquette - Leave No Trace

The *Leave No Trace Center for Outdoor Ethics* has created a set of guidelines to help minimize our impact on the places we hike and camp, and to assure that our wild places remain wild and pure for future generations.

Plan Ahead and Prepare

Travel and Camp on Durable Surfaces

Dispose of Waste Properly

Leave What You Find

Minimize Campfire Impacts

Respect Wildlife

Be Considerate of Other Visitors

Go to their website for more detailed information.
www.lnt.org/main.html

Some other things to think about

Urban backpacking

A good half of the trip is "urban backpacking". Urban backpacking routes weave through cities to find natural spots: parks, empty land, river corridors, rural roads, bike trails and the like that are the last havens for nature. Urban backpackers often find nature on an intimate scale: in a patch of oak hillside, a short stretch of shoreline, or a section of river corridor. Urban backpackers don't need to carry all the gear required in the wilderness; stores, restaurants and lodging are usually close at hand, and there is always the option to call a taxi or take a bus. If you are accustomed to hiking in the Sierra you may find urban backpacking strange at first. You won't be in remote wilderness with vast panoramic vistas of open space. Nor will you be alone in nature for days on end.

Urban backpacking has its own pleasures: it provides the opportunity to discover the wilderness in your own backyard. Even in the city, the beauty of nature is inspiring. Little pockets of nature like the determined blades of grass pushing up through the sidewalk below you, the gardens and landscape plantings bringing color to the buildings and roads beside you, and the swirling, billowing clouds and the soaring birds in the sky above you, can leave you as refreshed and inspired as Muir was in his beloved Yosemite.

Urban backpacking is a great group activity. One person walking through a city with a backpack may be perceived as a homeless person, and may be treated as someone to avoid or fear. When a group of people with backpacks walk through a city, it becomes a kind of movement, and people become curious, which leads to questions and the chance for education or interaction, and even the possibility of friendship or a request to join in.

The Muir Ramble Route as a "Green" vacation

Any time you vacation by walking, cycling or using public transportation, any time you camp or stay in locally owned hotels (local "eco-friendly" hotels are even better!) and eat at locally owned restaurants serving locally grown food, you are taking a "green" vacation. That vacation might be a weekend urban backpack trip, walking out your front door, seeking out the natural places and spending the night in a local campground or motel. It might be a trip using public transportation to get you and your bike to a distant starting point then enjoying the next several days' ride back home again.

We have devised walking routes through our town to go shopping, to go out to dinner or just to take long walks for exercise and relaxation. We follow the railroad tracks, stroll through parks, walk along suburban streets and cut through open lots. A green vacation can be as simple as finding satisfaction by immersing yourself in nature.

The MRR is not yet completely "green". Public transportation is not available to and from all the trailheads, and cars are required for shuttling in some places. But we hope one day, in the not too distant future, this will change. We hope the MRR will become a route for people to travel under their own power from the Bay Area to Yosemite, with B&Bs and hostels spaced every 10-15 miles.

Following the MRR, even as it exists today, is a good start towards taking a "green" vacation. You won't have to add hours of driving to a National Park destination just to begin your vacation. The California landscape will unfold at a human pace, just as it did for John Muir in 1868. You will see California in a way that is personal, historical and delightfully up close.

Make the history come alive

You are following Muir's footsteps. The MRR can be a walk through history. Most of the communities the MRR passes through have local history museums. Visit them, enjoy their displays and talk to the staff. Tell them what you are doing and talk to them about Muir's walk and California in Muir's time.

Another way to help bring the history alive is to read accounts of visits to California that were written in the 1860-70s. We suggest the following books: William Brewer's *Up and Down California* (1864) describes several of his trips made through the Santa Clara Valley and the Pacheco Pass area while mapping

California for the Whitney survey. In *A Journal of Rambling Through the High Sierra of California* (1874) Joseph LeConte tells the story of taking Berkeley students through the Sierra with Muir as their guide. Both James M. Hutchings' *Scenes of Wonder and Curiosity in California* and *Yosemite: Its Wonders and Its Beauties* (1868) by John S. Hittell, with photographs by Eadweard J. Muybridge describe how to get from Coulterville to Yosemite using the same route Muir used. John Olmsted also visited Yosemite in 1868 and wrote a book (now very rare but available on microfilm) titled: *A trip to California in 1868.* Another interesting work is *California: for Health, Pleasure and Residence,* by Charles Nordhoff (1872), and in 1876 Thompson and West published atlas maps of several counties Muir walked through.

We also recommend some more recent books including Jan Broek's *The Santa Clara Valley, California: A Study in Landscape Changes* (1932); *Santa Clara Valley: Images of the Past* (1977) by Donald DeMers; or *East Bay: Then and Now* (2004) by Dennis Evanosky. For the San Joaquin Valley we suggest *Ghost Towns of Merced County* (2005) by Herb Wood; and *The Road Over* (2002) by the Milliken Museum Society, available from the Merced County Courthouse Museum. For the foothills and Yosemite we recommend books available through the Yosemite Association, such as *Discovery of the Yosemite and the Indian War of 1851, which Led to that Event,* by Lafayette H. Bunnell (1911); *My First Summer in the Sierra* by John Muir (1911); or for some great historical photos of the area, read *Images of America: Yosemite National Park and Vicinity* by Leroy Radanovich (2006).

Disclaimer

The Muir Ramble Route is not yet an officially designated route. There are no trail markers for you to follow. Furthermore it is safe to say that the MRR really cannot be walked safely from beginning to end because there are places with no legal alternative but to walk on the narrow edge of busy highways. Highway walking, though legal, is dangerous and we recommend that you shuttle or take public transportation to pass through any dangerous sections of road on the MRR. Always use due caution in approaching undeveloped areas in urban situations; they are often used as dumping grounds, transient camps, and sites for illegal activity. The user is responsible for insuring the legality and safety of accessing all of the areas described along the MRR. The information and directions that follow are the result of our personal observations. The information has not been reviewed or approved by any park or government official. It reflects conditions and situations that may change at any time without notice. Hopefully all those changes will be for the better and soon it will be a designated trail without any of the current challenges.

De Anza College students urban backpacking through Newark

Muir Ramble Route:

San Francisco to Yosemite

in the Footsteps of John Muir

The Hiking Guide

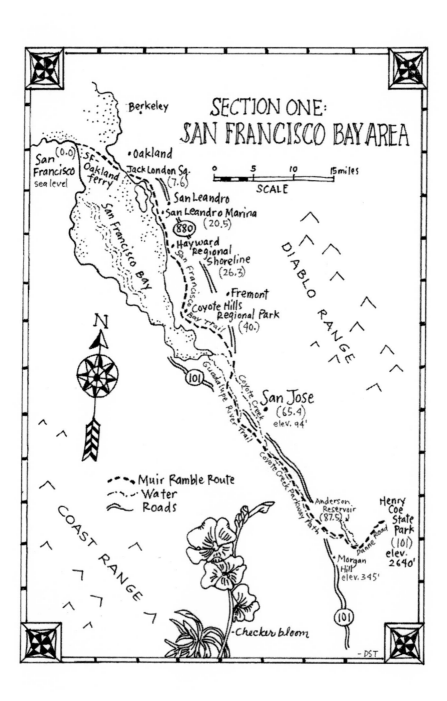

Section One: San Francisco Bay Area

Through Hike

Begin: The intersection of Davis St. and Broadway, San Francisco

End: Henry Coe State Park (HCSP) Ranch Headquarters, Morgan Hill

Distance: 101 miles

Section One of the MRR begins in San Francisco and ends just east of Morgan Hill at Henry Coe State Park. The trip starts crossing the Bay by ferry, passes through Jack London Square then heads south on the Bay Trail through Alameda County. The trip continues through Santa Clara County on bike trails and city streets following Coyote Creek and the Guadalupe River. It ends traveling a few miles east of Muir's actual route to access the wilderness preserved by the creation Henry

Following the Bay Trail through Oakland

Coe State Park. This is the most urban section of the Muir Ramble Route: about two thirds is through parks or on trails, the rest is on city streets and the contrast between the past and present is more obvious here than anywhere else on the MRR. It is also probably the easiest section to travel: the landscape is flat and the climate is more moderate than in any other section.

The Bay Trail is now about three-quarters complete, and when finished will be a 400-mile bike and walking path that circles the entire Bay. It is currently intermittent through Alameda County. Sometimes it wanders through the wilds of a shoreline park, or past flocks of shorebirds stalking in the bay's shallow tidelands, giving access to the Bay Area's wetlands; other times it follows city sidewalks or bike lanes past rangy industrial buildings and city streets. It finds access through hotels, condominium complexes and warehouses, using unlikely-looking paths or gravel roads, and reveals hidden panoramic views of the Bay, the Oakland hills and San Francisco's city skyline from these unusual vantage points. The Bay Trail's wanderings may cause the directions through Alameda County to seem very complicated, but when walking they are really very easy to follow and you can always just keep heading south like Muir did, staying between the Diablo and Coast ranges until they begin to come together near Gilroy.

The first time we rode this section on bikes we were joined by a Bay Area couple who had recently cycled in France. They enjoyed seeing the beauty of their own backyards, the shorebirds on the Bay, the vast landscapes of flowering fields in the valley and the oak-lined trails along the river bike trails. We bought wine and cheese in a little store for lunch, spent the nights in hotels and used public transportation to start and end the trip. The trip was a complete success and afterwards our friends even claimed that at a fraction of the cost the MRR rivaled their European cycling. Before this trip neither Donna or I had ridden more than ten miles in a day. But since the weather was mild, the landscape flat, the scenery engaging and the company enjoyable, it was no problem for us to pedal the 15–50 mile days, and we imagine any reasonably fit person with little cycling experience could do it too.

In 2008 we walked this section with a group of students from the Environmental Studies Department at De Anza College. They were working to assure that the Coyote Valley, near Morgan Hill, was preserved as open space for animals to migrate from the Santa Cruz Range to the Diablo Range, and planned the trip to culminate in a rally in Coyote Valley, where the public and the media could learn about their mission. It was a 5-day urban backpacking trip and we averaged 15 miles a day. Most of the students had never backpacked before and this was a seminal outdoor experience for them. We carried packs and slept in campgrounds, churches, shelters and private homes on or near the route. After the walk they gave a presentation to the student body, and what they shared gives a sense of their experience: "This MRR trail is more than recreational, it is a way to get from one place to another. One person with a backpack in the city is usually seen a vagrant, a danger, but ten people with backpacks becomes a kind of statement. A lot of people smiled when we hiked by. We inspired their imagination. We walked through a lot of amazing parks and beautiful open space. We even spent about a half of one day walking on city streets and some of the big ones didn't even have sidewalks. That was important in the context of the whole walk; to see how much land is dedicated to streets, business parks, housing tracts and auto malls and how little to nature and foot traffic. We experienced how hard it is for a person on foot to get from one place to another because of all the freeways and bridges and buildings. Think how much harder it must be for the animals that want to migrate."

Recommended Trip

Begin: Oakland's Clay St. ferry landing, near Jack London Square. (MRR mile 7.6)

End: Terminus of the Coyote Creek Bikeway in Morgan Hill. (MRR mile 86.9)

Distance: 79.3 miles

The recommended trip begins in Oakland at the modern ferry landing near Jack London Square. It ends at the south terminus of the Coyote Creek Trail near Anderson County Park in Morgan Hill. You could, like Muir, start in San Francisco, but the added logistics make it hard to recommend this for the person with limited time. The trip can be done as a 2 or 3-day bike ride or a 6-day walk. We recommend you use public transportation and make it a round trip. Just leave your car at the Fremont Bay Area Rapid Transit (BART) station, take BART to Oakland, walk or cycle to Morgan Hill, and then take a bus back to the Fremont BART station.

The route follows the Bay Trail through Alameda County. Just before entering Santa Clara County a one-mile section of trail that will cross the river drainage between Fremont Blvd. and Dixon Landing Rd. has not yet been completed. This is scheduled to be complete in the not too distant future, but until then you will have to either illegally forge through the muddy wet-lands or make a 4.9-mile detour through Warm Springs on city streets. It is a very nice bike ride, but a lot of extra miles to walk.

The route continues through Santa Clara County following the Coyote Creek Bike Path along the sycamore and cottonwood-lined riparian river corridor, then on city streets through business parks near the airport, then connects with the Guadalupe River Trail which ends in downtown San Jose. The MRR crosses downtown San Jose from west to east on city streets then connects up with the Coyote Creek Trail, an 18 mile bike path that follows along the wonderfully still natural and richly verdant Coyote Creek river corridor to its southern trailhead in Morgan Hill.

If you take the recommended trip on a bicycle we suggest you leave from Oakland after work on a Friday. That makes day one an easy 13-mile ride to a hotel at the San Leandro Marina. Day two is a 42-mile ride to downtown San Jose where there are many hotel options. The third day is a 20-mile ride to the end of the Coyote Creek Trail in Morgan Hill and there will be plenty of time to take public transportation back to the beginning trailhead. Experienced street riders often peddle up to Henry Coe State Park for exercise so we recommend the trip up Dunne Road for the serious cyclist only.

This also makes a wonderful and challenging 6-day walking trip. We recommend you leave early the first day and a 13-mile walk will get you to the San Leandro Marina Inn. On the second day an 18-mile walk will get you to the campground at the Coyote Hills. On the third day a 10-mile walk will get you to a hotel right on the route in Hayward. If you don't want to camp, this could be done as two 14-mile days, staying in a hotel less than a mile from the route in the Union City region of Fremont. On the fourth day a 16-mile walk will get you to downtown San Jose (this will be about 4 miles shorter when the detour is eliminated). On the fifth day a 10-mile walk will get you to a hotel on Silicon Valley Blvd. The last day is an easy 10-mile walk to the ending trailhead in Morgan Hill, and if you leave early there will be plenty of time to take a taxi to the bus stop and the bus back to the BART station. East Dunne Road is steep, small and winding and we do not recommend walking up to Henry Coe State Park.

What you need and need to know

Maps:

Street Maps: AAA City Series. Oakland-Berkeley, Hayward-San Leandro, Fremont-Union City, Sunnyvale-Santa Clara-Western San Jose, San Jose Eastern & Central Bay, Gilroy-Morgan Hill.

San Francisco Bay Trail Maps: East Bay-Richmond to Hayward, South Bay - Redwood Shores to Newark. Look online for ordering info.

Coyote Creek and Guadalupe River Trail Maps: look online for printable maps.

Park Maps: Santa Clara County Parks Map: Anderson County Park. Henry Coe State Park map available through the Pine Ridge Association website online.

Accommodations:

There are many hotels in the metropolitan areas adjacent to the route and these can be located by Internet searches. The lodging for the recommended trips are noted in the directions then, listed as resources at the end of the section. There is camping at Coyote Hills Regional Park (groups only) and at Henry Coe State Park.

Food and Water:

Carry food and water with you. There are a few stores directly on the route, and more can usually be found within a mile or so from the trail. There are water fountains and rest rooms in every park the route passes through, but they may not all be in service.

Section One Trailhead Information

Through Hike Beginning Trailhead:

Access by Car: Exit Highway 80 at the Fremont St exit. Go 0.5 mile. Keep right at the fork, follow signs for Folsom St. Turn left at Folsom St. Go 0.3 mile. Turn left at the Embarcadero.

Go 0.7 mile. Turn left on Broadway. Go 1 block to Davis and Broadway.

Access by Public Transportation: SF Muni bus #12 goes to Jack London Square.

Ending Trailhead:

Access by Car: Exit Highway 101 on East Dunne Road and follow it east for 12 miles, to its end at the Coe Ranch Headquarters.

Access by Public Transportation: Yellow Cab Taxi Service

Recommended Trip Beginning Trailhead:

Access by Car: Exit Interstate 880 on the Broadway/ Alameda exit. Follow the signs to Jack London Square. Go 0.2 mile west on Broadway. Turn right Second St. Go 0.1 mile. Turn left on Clay St. Go 0.1 mile to the ferry terminal. There is pay parking available in nearby garages.

Access by Public Transportation: Take BART to the 12th St. Oakland City Center station. Exit the station and travel west on Broadway. Go 0.6 mile into Jack London Square. We recommend beginning and ending at the Fremont BART station. They have a place for extended parking and it is free on the weekends. You will need to talk to the station manger to verify the location of extended parking and which BART car to use when you have a bike.

Ending Trailhead:

Access by Car: Exit Highway 101 on Cochrane Rd. in Morgan Hill. Head northeast. Go 1.1 miles. Turn left on Malaguerra Ave. Go 0.3 mile. Turn left Morning Star Dr. Go 0.05 mile to Eagle View Dr. There is day parking near the park headquarters at the end of Malaguerra, and parking is allowed on city streets in Morgan Hill for up to 3 consecutive days.

Access by Public Transportation: Yellow Cab Taxi.

Note: If you are taking the Recommended Trip using BART, see mile 86.9 for directions for returning to the Fremont BART Station from the ending trailhead.

Section One Directions

(0.0) The Muir Ramble Route begins in San Francisco at the intersection of Davis and Broadway Streets. Head east on Broadway. Go 1 block.

Note: This is where the Francisco-Oakland Railroad's ferry terminal was located in 1868. Since then the Bay has been filled in, and this is now a full city block from the water.

(0.1) Turn right on Embarcadero. Go 0.4 mile.

(0.5) Turn left into the Ferry Plaza. Go 0.1 mile, past the Ferry Building to South terminal Gate E.

(0.6) Take the Oakland/Alameda ferry, traveling to Jack London Square, 7 miles across the Bay. The first stop is in Alameda. Get off at the second stop which is in Oakland at the end of Clay St., near Jack London Square.

Note: Look online for schedules and fares. Bikes are allowed on the ferry.

(7.6) Leave the Oakland ferry landing at the end of Clay St. Go one hundred feet to the intersection of Clay and Water St.

Note: This is the trailhead for the suggested bike and walking trips. In 1868 the Oakland terminal was near present day 7th and Wood Streets. The shoreline was so shallow that the SF-Oakland RR had constructed a wharf stretching three-quarters of a mile into the Bay to avoid the problems caused by tidal changes. Passengers and goods were loaded on a train that took them down the wharf and into Oakland. There was a West Oakland station near the terminus, a stop at West

San Francisco Ferry Building to Oakland
(0.0 – 8.6)

Muir began his trip "on or about the first of April" by taking the ferry to Oakland, and we did the same. Despite the drizzly morning, thirty people were waiting for us at the ferry terminal to see us off. Some were friends and family but a significant number were people we didn't know, who came after reading the front-page article (the "Local" section) about us that morning in the San Francisco Chronicle. We spoke a few words about the journey ahead, sang a rousing song for the road and people cheered us on!

When we got to Oakland we were welcomed and then led to the Bay Trail by a woman who had also read about our trek in the Chronicle. If she had not been there to show us the dockside promenade we would have just followed the "first road we came to" as Muir had, and missed the Bay Trail completely. We followed the blue and white Bay Trail signs for several miles, past marinas, through parks, past barb wired warehouses and looming industrial buildings. Clouds darkened the sky and we were happy we had only planned to walk a short distance the first day. The sky let loose. We ended the first day running for a BART station in the pouring rain.

Oakland to San Leandro
(8.6 – 18.2)

It was still raining so we put up umbrellas and started

Martin Luther King, Jr. Regional Shoreline

7th St. and Broadway and then a stop called "Brooklyn", near the intersection of 14th St. and 14th Ave. Muir states he left the train in East Oakland, so we believe Muir did not get off at 7th and Broadway, and that the "first road he came to" was 14th St.

(7.6) Turn right. Go 1 mile, continuing south, past Jack London Square and through Estuary Park.

Note: Jack London didn't spend time here until the 1880s, and in Muir's day the area was just docks and shipyards. As you head south along Water St. look to your right for blue and white enamel signs that say "San Francisco Bay Trail" (BT). These signs will lead you off Water St. on the BT's intermittent dockside trail. Look for those Bay Trail signs! Estuary Park has picnic grounds and restrooms.

(8.6) Turn right on Embarcadero Ave. Go 0.7 mile, using sidewalks or the bike lane.

(9.3) Turn right on 10th St. Go 0.1 mile, cutting through the Hilton Hotel's parking lot to another section of the BT beside the Bay.

(9.4) Turn left. Go 0.4 mile, following the BT south, past the hotel, until it ends at Marine Max.

(9.8) Turn left. Go 0.1 mile, returning to Embarcadero.

(9.9) Turn right. Go 0.1 mile, stop just before reaching the Executive Inn Suites.

(10.0) Turn right. Go 200 feet, following the BT to the bay.

(10.0) Turn left. Go 0.4 mile following the BT, between the hotel and the water, till it ends in the Embarcadero Cove Marina.

(10.4) Turn left. Go 200 feet, through the buildings and parking lot, back to Embarcadero.

(10.4) Turn right on Embarcadero. Go 0.2 mile, stopping just past the intersection with Livingston St. on the left.

(10.6) Turn right onto the BT. Go 0.3 mile following it around to the south until it ends at Dennison.

(10.9) Turn left. Go 0.1 mile, returning to Embarcadero.

(11.0) Turn right. Go 0.5 mile following Embarcadero past Union Point Park.

Note: The park is landscaped with native plants, architecturally interesting play areas and sculptures. There is water and there are restrooms. On some maps Embarcadero becomes E. 7th St. after the park.

(11.5) Turn right on Kennedy St. Go 0.2 mile.

Note: A sign indicates this turn as the bike route to Alameda.

(11.7) Angle to the right onto 23rd St. Go 0.1 mile, to a multiple street intersection.

(11.8) Turn right, cross 29th Ave. and continue on Glascock St. Go 100 feet to the BT sign on a gate for the Waterpark Lofts.

walking through Oakland. The rain didn't bother us too much since we both had good rain pants and rainproof jackets complements of Patagonia. It was about 55 degrees, but we kept warm as long as we kept walking. The adventure would continue, rain or not. We had created our parallel route with the hope that we would find more natural beauty than if we were following Muir's actual footsteps on modern roads, but here the Bay Trail was a study in contrasts: first it followed city streets with sprawling old factories and barbed wire lined sidewalks, then it led us down rural bayside trails with birds hunting for food in the tidewaters and breathtaking views across the water.

I decided I should walk as if I were no longer Peter Thomas, but rather John Muir, who was always ecstatic about the plants he saw. It proved great fun. The first wildflower I saw was a purple one. That's all I knew. Donna told me it was a malva rosa. Looking with my new "John Muir" eyes, I saw the beauty: the petals were rich shades of pink and purple with reddish stripes at the center of each petal, and in the middle of the flower was a coral dot over an ivory pad. These were color combinations only an artist would imagine together. I thought the dot was a pistil, and I wondered if Muir would have said I was on road to perdition, staring at the sex part of the plant. Donna said she thought Muir would have seen it as part of a plant, a perfect expression of God's beauty and would have applauded me for looking so closely.

Late that night, staying at a friend's house, we checked our email. We thought about John Muir: he did not received a single letter on his trip, and any letters he wrote must have been lost, because his family in Wisconsin worried he was dead. We were pleased to find messages from well-wishers and even requests from reporters interested in a story. But the email was not all fan mail. One note, sent by a fellow who signed himself Fred C. Dobbs (Dobbs was the curmudgeon in *The Treasure of the Sierra Madre*) went as follows:

"I gather you have no intention of walking Mr. Muir's 1868 way from Oakland to San Jose. The way he took is still there: 14th Street Oakland, Mission Boulevard, Warm Springs Road, Milpitas Road, Oakland Avenue. It being public, no private permission is necessary. What is the point of walking the Bay Trail when Muir did not and would not have taken it, it being impassable and mostly underwater in those days?"

The email caused all the insecurities and worries we had to surface again. Were we doing the right thing, the "John Muir" thing, by following the Bay Trail instead of the modern roads that traced the actual route Muir used? Was the most important point of this trip really to see what Muir might have seen and to note what has changed? We

(11.8) Turn right. Go 0.2 mile, passing through the Lofts' courtyard, then continue south on the BT until it ends on an unnamed parking street, an extension of Derby Ave., near the Oakland Museum Warehouse.

(12.0) Turn left. Go 250 feet, back to Glascock St.

(12.1) Turn right. Go 0.1 mile.

(12.2) Cross Lancaster St. Go 0.1 mile, following abandoned railroad tracks to unsigned Fruitvale Ave.

(12.3) Turn right. Go 0.1 mile, stopping just before the bridge.

(12.4) Turn left on Alameda Ave. Go 0.3 mile, initially beside the water, to the first driveway after the road curves to the left (east).

(12.7) Turn right. Go 0.1 mile passing through the warehouse parking lot towards the Bay and another section of Bay Trail.

(12.8) Turn left on the BT. Go 0.3 mile until the BT ends at High St.

(13.1) Turn left, then immediately right on Tidewater Ave. Go 0.2 mile stopping just before a stop sign for Lesser St. on the left.

(13.3) Turn right and enter the Martin Luther King, Jr. Regional Shoreline. Go 0.7 mile following the BT south along the Bay until just after it turns inland at an unnamed drainage entering the Bay.

Note: The Martin Luther King, Jr. Regional Shoreline, part of the East Bay Regional Parks, wraps around the edge of San Leandro Bay. Its extensive and protected marshlands provide a stopover for migrating birds on the Pacific Flyway. The park has picnic facilities, drinking water, restrooms, a sunbathing beach and children's play areas.

(14.0) Turn right, cross the bridge, turn right again and stay near the water's edge. Go 0.7 mile.

(14.7) Cross a bridge over the Damon Slough then turn right. Go 0.8 mile, following the Garretson Point Trail, past picnic tables, water and restrooms.

(15.5) Cross the bridge over Elmhurst Creek then turn right. Go 0.1 mile following the water's edge.

(15.6) Cross the bridge over San Leandro Creek then turn right. Go 1.1 mile along the Arrowhead Marsh Trail, past the observation tower and restored marsh areas.

(16.7) The path ends. Turn left on Doolittle Dr. Go 1.5 miles.

Note: You are near the Oakland International Airport with hotels and restaurants close by.

(18.2) Turn right on Davis St. Go 0.5 mile.

(18.7) Stay straight, past the Davis St. Station for Materials Recycling on your left. Pass through or around the sometimes-locked chain-link gate and go 1.2 miles.

Note: The gate is signed "Authorized Personnel Only", but this is actually the back entrance to the Oyster Bay Regional Shoreline, a 157-acre park built on a landfill that was closed in the early 1980s. The Bay Trail runs around the edge of the park in a semicircle along the Bay, and

decided to check to see if we had made a mistake. We drove over to East 14th street then followed it south towards Mission Boulevard. The roads Muir followed were still main thoroughfares, now lined with little shops and businesses. We tried to imagine if this would be better: window-shopping our way to Yosemite. But nature was hidden from view. That cinched it for us. We knew we had made the Muir-like decision; the right one for us, even though the Bay Trail was pocked by industrial areas it would be the route that would lead us past more plants, more birds, and more "anywhere that is wild."

San Leandro to San Lorenzo (18.2 – 26.3)

We started walking in the pouring rain. Huge trucks sped by spraying showers of puddle water over the sidewalk, thoroughly drenching us. It was hard to think about the trip being a "fun adventure" at this point. It just felt grueling. After a half-mile we found a sign for the Bay Trail directing us down a dirt road that was also the entrance to the regional recycling plant. Here the trail was built over San Leandro's reclaimed dump lands. As we walked through the pouring rain we watched shore birds hunt for food in vast piles of recyclable plastic and metal.

The wind picked up and made our umbrellas useless. We cinched down our rain gear and kept walking. There were wonderful, vast stormy views of the coastal wetlands. The wind whipped up raindrops that played with the light shining from between the clouds. The Bay was a patchwork of grey, blue and black. The shoreline was beautiful in the storm, the low tide puddles glistening with rainwater and the marsh a field of mud speckled with driftwood and busy shorebirds.

The trail was an industrial archeologist's dream. Here and there an old crumbling pier extended out to deeper water. In Muir's day these had been used for the extensive shipping done on the Bay. Beside the graveled walkway rusty pipe and bits of machinery were jammed between chunks of concrete rubble. Some of the rubble was clearly from the 1906 earthquake, bits of rounded Victorian shapes from the walls and facades of old buildings. Other bits were clearly modern: straight-sided chunks from curbs and gutters with names and dates stamped in them. When Muir made his walk there had been huge shell mounds in the area, piles of clam, mussel, and oyster shells cast off by the early Native American inhabitants. Those mounds had been mostly leveled by the 1920s, used to make concrete, and that concrete had ended up back here again: shells could often be seen in chunks of trailside rubble.

We got to our car around 3 pm and drove to a cafe where we relaxed with a warm cup of tea. I asked Donna what she

the views are spectacular. Picnic sites are located on the hill. Water and restrooms are located at the southern entrance on Neptune Dr. Marsh hawks, black-shouldered kites, red-tailed hawks, and shorebirds abound in this East Bay Regional Park.

(19.9) The Shoreline Trail ends. Turn right on Neptune Dr. Go 0.6 mile.

(20.5) Turn right on Monarch Bay Dr. Go 0.7 mile, continuing past the San Leandro Marina and the Shoreline Recreation Area, stopping when the street ends at a golf course.

Note: You will pass the San Leandro Marina Inn, a good place to spend the night. Two restaurants are steps away, and there is a spot tucked behind the inn to lock up bikes for the night. Breakfast is included in the price. The San Leandro Shoreline Recreation Area, managed by the city of San Leandro, has great walking trails. It also has play areas, picnic tables, restrooms and water.

(21.2) Veer right onto a pedestrian path. Go 2 miles, crossing a bridge over Estudillo Flood Control Canal and following the BT along a bike path between a golf course and the water.

Note: This bike path passes through the restored marshland areas of San Leandro. Miles and half-miles are painted on the pavement.

(23.2) Turn right at the Heron Bay signpost. Go 0.7 mile, passing between a large housing subdivision and the tidal wetlands, turning right when you come to the San Lorenzo Creek.

(23.9) Turn left and cross the creek on a wooden bridge. Go 2.4 miles, staying close the water's edge on the BT as it crosses Bockman Channel, Sulpher Creek and a flood control channel then turns inland to circle around Cogswell Marsh.

Hayward Regional Shoreline

Note: You are now in the Hayward Regional Shoreline, a 1,713 acre park that is part of the East Bay Regional Parks. The tidal marshlands were used by Native Americans to harvest salt and in 1868 there were 18 small commercial salt production operations between here and Alameda Creek, which runs just north of Coyote Hills. You will be passing remnants of those salt ponds and the landings used to ferry goods to San Francisco.

(26.3) Turn right at an intersection where you see a City of Hayward "No Trespassing" sign posted straight ahead. Go 2.2 miles, staying near the Bay until the trail turns inland to reach the Shoreline's trailhead near the Hayward Regional Shoreline Interpretive Center.

Note: 0.4 mile after crossing a bridge over Cogswell Marsh the trail splits. Take either fork; both end at the same place. The Interpretive Center has displays of the natural and cultural history of the area, restrooms and water.

(28.5) Turn left onto the freeway frontage road. Go 0.3 mile.

thought Muir would have been doing. "Muir would have walked until dark, then just slept on the ground, or begged a dry bed in a barn. But if we try that we will probably get rousted by police, so I think we better just call some friends and see if we can spend the night."

San Lorenzo to Coyote Hills (26.3 - 39.5)

Katy Sommer, one of Donna's backpacking buddies, met us at our trailhead and hiked with us for the day. She was six months pregnant but that didn't slow her down. I kept falling behind as she and Donna walked and talked at a mile-a-minute pace. For the first few miles we walked through wetlands, bird-watching our way along the muddy path. This section of the Bay Trail is a prime habitat for resident and migrating birds: spotted sandpipers bobbed at the shore, avocets, with their upward-curved bills, waded in the shallows and killdeer called out their warnings in shrill voices. A snowy egret, with its flyaway white feathers, stood in the shallows and a graceful necked grebe dove in deeper water for small fish.

I told Katy about putting on Muir eyes. She tried it too and together we studied beautiful tiny little wildflowers, ones we never would have noticed otherwise. Few were natives, but we didn't let that stop us from enjoying the purple and pink colors they added to the otherwise green landscape. The region was pretty flat, so we could see a long way, and in the distance to the south we could see the green Coyote Hills poking up over the marshlands. All day we watched them grow bigger as they got closer. Looking backwards, up the Bay, we could see San Francisco and Oakland getting smaller, further away. I was experiencing one of the great pleasures of long distance walking, to see your goal get closer and the places you have been recede in the distance.

We ended the day in the lush green of Coyote Hills Regional Park. It is a haven for nature, with tidal wetlands, green grasslands and oak-studded rolling hills. The park has only one campsite, and it is for groups, but they decided we could be called a small "hiking club" and allowed us to spend the night. The campsite was a grassy paradise nestled in a small valley under a looming green promontory featuring a large rock outcropping, with

(28.8) Turn left at the entrance to the pedestrian bridge. Go 0.2 mile, crossing south over Highway 92.

(29.0) Turn left, heading east on an unsigned city street (Point Eden Way). Go 0.4 mile.

Note: You are now in what is ironically called a business "park".

(29.4) Turn right on Eden Landing Rd. Go 0.2 mile.

(29.6) Turn left on Arden Rd. Go 1.2 mile.

(30.8) Arden curves left and becomes Baumberg Ave. Go 0.2 mile.

Note: Straight ahead is the entrance for the Eden Landing Ecological Reserve, a shorebird refuge. When the Bay Trail is complete it will travel from here south through the Reserve.

(31.0) After crossing the railroad tracks, turn right on Industrial Blvd. Go 0.5 mile.

Note: If you are not camping at Coyote Hills, the Phoenix Lodge is 0.8 mile ahead on Industrial Parkway West.

(31.5) Turn right on Marina Dr. Go 0.5 mile (2 blocks).

(32.0) Turn left on Eden Park Place. Go 0.2 mile (1 block).

(32.2) Turn right on Hesperian Blvd. Go 3.8 miles.

Note: Hesperian becomes Union City Blvd. after crossing Alameda Creek. At Smith St. it is the main street of the former town of Alvarado, and there are shops with food to the east.

(36.0) Cross the bridge over the Alameda County Flood Control Channel (the safest place for pedestrians to walk may be on the center divider). Turn right and enter the Coyote Hills Regional Park. Go 1.8 miles following the Alameda Creek Trail parallel to the flood control channel.

Note: The Coyote Hills Regional Park is nearly 1000 acres of marshland and rolling grassland-covered hills. There are boardwalks winding through the wildlife-rich wetlands, and you can hike to the top of one of the peaks here for great views in all directions. It has a campsite, the first on the route! The campsite is for groups only, so call yourself a group and reserve it through the East Bay Regional Park District office.

(37.8) At the northern foot of Coyote Hills turn left and go up the hill on a connector trail. Take the next right, which is the Bayview Trail. Go 1.7 miles to the west and then south, wrapping around the hills for some fantastic views of the Bay.

(39.5) At the fourth trail junction turn right on the Apay Way. (Continuing straight ahead will take you to the Dairy Glen group camp). Go 0.5 mile.

Note: The trail name changes to the Quarry Trail as it winds up towards Highway 84 and passes the old gravel quarry. City plans are to reclaim this quarry for a public campground.

(40.0) After passing the quarry, the trail splits. Stay left for better views. Go 0.5 mile.

(40.5) The Coyote Hill bike trail ends. Cross Highway 84 on a pedestrian bridge. Turn right onto a park service road, then left (south) onto unsigned Marshlands

small pond and marsh below and to the south. In the midst of the busy East Bay we had the whole park to ourselves and fell to sleep to the quiet sounds of birds, the wind rustling the reeds of the pond.

Coyote Hills to Fremont (39.5 – 49.4)

A reporter from the Fremont Argus, Jonathan Jones, had contacted us to write a story about our walk and so hiked with us for a few hours. We left the campsite following a bucolic sunlit trail lined with brilliant green grass and glowing orange poppies. Jones could not believe such an idyllic place existed in his own backyard.

We talked about Muir, who loved Yosemite and did everything he could to see it protected as a National Park. Why would anyone want to conserve a place of natural beauty like Coyote Hills? Because they love it enough to want to do something. It is all about love. What will make the people of Alameda and Santa Clara County want a complete Bay Trail? Get them out on it. Once they have seen the beauty, completing the trail will seem logical rather than fanatical.

The park trail ended and we walked on city streets along a narrow road used by 18-wheelers. There was no curb, sidewalk or shoulder. This was probably the scariest stretch of road we had walked, and that made good copy for Jonathan, but we got off the road ASAP.

Good copy or not, we weren't looking to die there. Jones left us and we took a sort of slow shortcut, following railroad tracks for several hours. It was hard to step tie to tie, and equally hard to crunch over the gravel beside the rails and we gained respect for the hobos of yore. We left the rails on a trash-lined, shoulder-less road that led from the dump to new business parks, with green grassy lawns, ornamental flowering shrubs and curving sidewalks. That was the first time we admitted to enjoying sidewalks, but only because they were so easy to walk on after all those miles on slanting gravel and uneven railroad ties. At the end of the day Jonathan Jones picked us up and took us back to Coyote Hills for another night of camping.

Fremont to Milpitas
(49.4 – 55.7)

We woke up in a cloudy paradise, surrounded by the hills, marshes and birds of Coyote Hills Park. I was amazed at how "Muir-like" I was becoming: I noticed the weather and looked forward to spending the whole day outside walking. Today we had to cross the Coyote Creek. It drains into the bay between Fremont and Milpitas. Muir's Oakland Rd. had crossed it with a bridge, but our incomplete Bay Trail does not have an official way to cross it. On reconnaissance before the trip we had thought it possible to ford the creek then cut cross-country through marshland to Dixon Landing, but because of the recent rain the storm ditch

Rd. Go 0.1 mile, past the Newark Slough Learning Center parking lot, to the Don Edwards San Francisco Bay National Wildlife Refuge visitor center parking lot on the right.

Note: The wild area to the west of Marshlands Rd. and south of the freeway is part of the Don Edwards San Francisco Bay National Wildlife Refuge, a huge refuge that encompasses 30,000 acres of mudflats, salt marshes, open land and bay.

(40.6) Turn right on the unsigned Tidelands Trail. Go 0.2 mile, past the visitor center, up to the Hilltop Overlook.

Note: The visitor center has both historical information panels and natural history displays. Open Tuesday through Sunday, 10:00 a.m. to 5:00 p.m. From the overlook you can see south all the way to Gilroy. Note how the Diablo and Santa Cruz mountain ranges come together, just as Muir described in his account.

(40.8) Continue down the Tidelines Trail 0.3 mile.

(41.1) Make a sharp left turn on Harrier Trail. Go 0.3 mile.

(41.4) Turn right on an unsigned paved county road (Marshlands Rd). Go 0.3 mile.

(41.7) Turn right on Thornton Ave. Go 1.9 miles.

Note: On a busy road like this that does not have bike lanes or sidewalks, walk on the left side of the road, facing the traffic, and cycle on the right, with the flow of traffic, claiming the full right lane when there is no shoulder. There is currently no alternative for the MRR but

Cogswell Marsh, Hayward Regional Shoreline

to follow busy city streets for the next 5.8 miles. It is a fine bike ride, but if walking you might want to consider taking a bus or taxi. The closest bus stop is at Thornton Ave. and Sycamore St. Take AC Transit bus #214 to the Fremont BART station, then the #212 south to Fremont Blvd and Cushing Parkway, about a one hour trip.

(43.6) Turn right on Cherry St. Go 1.6 miles.

Note: Cherry becomes Boyce Rd. at Stevenson Blvd, then Cushing Parkway at Auto Mall Blvd.

(45.2) Cross Mowry Blvd. Go 4.2 miles.

Note: The Newark Sportsfield Park, with restrooms and water, is on the right. Although Newark has miles of wetlands that could have trails this is currently the only large park in the city.

for Agua Fria Creek was running too high and fast to safely cross, so we were going to have to make a five-mile detour east then south through the city. The only good we could see in this was it gave us a chance to walk the actual road Muir would have taken.

The Oakland Road may have been beautiful in Muir's time but not anymore, at least not to us, looking for traces of nature, and we soon had enough of walking on Muir's actual route. In every direction except straight up we saw evidence of humans: grey asphalt, manicured monocultures of lawns, cement buildings, metal road signs, housing tracts, strip malls and apartment complexes. We couldn't get

Coyote Creek Lagoon Day Use Area, Fremont

(49.4) Turn right on FremontBlvd Go 0.7 mile.

Note: There is a Good Nite Inn and food at the corner of Cushing Parkway and Fremont Blvd. and is a convenient place to spend the night.

(50.1) Turn right on an unmarked gravel service road, just before the first signal at West Warren. Go 0.2 mile.

(50.3) Turn left on a second gravel road, just before reaching a small city park. (No water or restrooms.) Go 0.3 mile.

Note: This is the northern trailhead for the Coyote Creek Lagoon day use area, where the BT follows jogging trails along its levees. It is 260 acres of restored marsh, including a 25 acre native pickleweed stand. The wetland views are stunning, and surprising given the industrial surroundings.

(50.6) Turn left at a T junction. Go 1.4 miles.

(52.0) Turn left at a T junction. Go 0.4 mile.

(52.4) Turn right and cross the slough. Go 1 mile, following the Bay Trail south to the intersection of Dixon Landing Rd. and McCarthy Blvd.

Note: The section of Bay Trail between Fremont Blvd. and Dixon Landing Rd. is scheduled to be completed by the end of 2010. If it is not then you will have to take a 4.9 mile detour on city streets, a nice bike ride, but a half days walk. Detour

out of there fast enough. We used Dixon Landing Road to cross over Interstate 880, then connected with the Bay Trail again as it followed the Coyote Creek Bike Path along the Coyote Creek. Here the creek was lined with tall cottonwood and sycamore trees and thick willow underbrush, an urban haven for homeless animals and plants displaced by the onslaught of development. We stopped to rest; a red tail hawk landed on top of the tallest dead tree in sight and called out to its mate. There had not yet been many chances to botanize, but the opportunities for bird watching certainly made up for that.

We ended the day walking through more business complexes looking for the light rail station. So many of the huge buildings were completely vacant. Donna noted the irony Muir might have seen: where in the recent past there were vacant fields, directions: Take Fremont Blvd. back to Cushing Parkway. Go 2.2 miles.

Cross over Highway 880 on Fremont Blvd. Go 0.6 mile.

Turn right on Industrial Dr. Go 50 yards.

Turn right on Kato Rd., sandwiched between the New United Motor Manufacturing (NUMMI) plant and Highway 880. Go 3.4 miles, staying on Kato Rd. as it crosses Mission Blvd. and continues parallel to Interstate Highway 880.

Turn right on Milmont Drive. Go 0.5 mile.

Turn right on Dixon Landing Rd. Go 0.6 mile, crossing over Highway 880.

Turn left on McCarthy Blvd.

(53.4) Pass the entrance for the dump. Go 0.2 mile following McCarthy Blvd. to the left over Coyote Creek.

(53.6) Turn right immediately after crossing the second bridge at the signed entrance for the Coyote Creek Bike Trail. Go 1.8 miles, following the trail south.

Note: This terminus of the Coyote Creek is the beginning of our ramble on the Coyote Creek Bike Path, on the San Francisco Bay Trail, in the city of Milpitas. The creek is to the west of the bike path and is often hidden by the sycamores and willows that are home to many nesting birds in the spring.

(55.4) The Coyote Creek Bike Trail ends just west of the McCarthy Ranch Shopping Center. Turn left, go through the parking area, turn right on McCarthy Blvd. and go 0.3 mile, crossing over Highway 237.

now there were a bunch of vacant buildings instead.

Milpitas to San Jose
(55.7 – 61.1)

As we followed the landscaped sidewalks of yet another business park, I asked Donna what she thought Muir would have said about of all the flower-scapes we were passing. She said Muir probably would have preferred wildness and weeds. My John Muir eyes agreed: when I saw a little weed growing through a crack in the pavement, or in a neglected corner of a parking lot, I found myself smiling and silently cheering it on.

We ended the day at a light rail station, took public transportation back to our VW in Milpitas and spent the night on a quiet neighborhood street nearby.

San Jose
(61.1 – 65.4)

We followed the Guadalupe River Trail into San Jose. The sky was wild with clouds and light, grey, blue, black and gold swirled above us. The wind blew across the long green grass beside the trail. Donna pointed to a duck diving in the creek, but it never surfaced, and then we saw it was really a huge salmon. We watched it swim lazy circles in the muddy water, making its way slowly upstream. High above in the huge cottonwoods there were great blue herons, nesting, squawking to each other and spreading news of our approach from tree to tree.

The trail crossed the river several times. At one point it was unclear which side we should be on. We saw a man ahead of us cutting around a fence. Assuming this was a short cut, we followed him into a lush field and soon were up to our waists in weeds, mostly radish and mustard with a few native purple arroyo lupines poking their heads above the tall non-natives. This was clearly not the main trail but we were sure Muir would have loved it. We certainly did. Donna got excited as she talked about how a faint trail in the Sierra Nevada often indicated a secret route to somewhere special. We plowed through the weeds and ended up in a flooded and abandoned homeless camp. It was a secret route, but not to a place we wanted.

San Jose to Almaden
(65.4 – 72.3)

We walked through downtown San Jose, just as Muir did on his way to Yosemite. We stopped at the University library to give another presentation about Muir and our Trans-California Ramble then continued walking. A bike trail, following the Coyote Creek all the way to Morgan Hill, began a few miles south of downtown. Surely, we thought, we can find a way to avoid walking on city streets to get there. In the empty fields to the east of Kelley Park we could see trees marking the path of the creek, so we cut through the field, hoping to find a way to follow the creek south to the trailhead. A faint trail

(55.7) Turn right on the Highway 237 Bikeway, a highway frontage road for bikes and pedestrians. Go 0.3 mile.

(56.0) Turn left after crossing Coyote Creek, pass through a chain link gate and immediately turn right onto the dirt road. Go 3.4 miles.

Note: This is a section of the Coyote Creek Bike Trail. It follows maintenance roads along the creek's west bank. The low road, being closer to the river, is better for walking.

(59.4) Before the second bridge, leave the trail to the right. Turn right on the Montague Expressway. Go   0.3 mile.

Note: It appears you could continue straight ahead on the trail, and perhaps you will see other walkers or cyclists doing this, but public access is not permitted on the maintenance road south of Montague Expressway, and will not get you where you want to go.

(59.7) Turn left at the first signal, which is East Trimble Rd. (confusingly signed on the right for a business as "Cadence"). Go 1.4 miles.

(61.1) Just before crossing the Guadalupe River turn right to access the Guadalupe River Trail. Follow a bike trail for a hundred feet then cut back left. Go south 1.3 miles, passing under Trimble and following the trail on the east side of the river.

Note: The Guadalupe River Trail, managed by San Jose City Parks, follows the river for 11 miles, from Alviso to Lake Almaden Park.

(62.4) Cross to the west side of the river at Airport Parkway. Go 2 miles, following the trail south into the Guadalupe River Park.

(64.4) Just before Coleman Ave., when the trail splits in two, take the right fork (just past a rock wall on the west side of the trail). Go 100 feet.

(64.4) Turn left on Coleman Ave., cross the bridge and continue south following the trail on the east side of the river. Go 1 mile.

(65.4) Turn left on Santa Clara St. Go 0.4 mile.

Note: This is the old downtown San Jose. In the California History room of the MLK public library there are photographs on the wall taken here in 1868. Downtown has good places to eat and spend the night. The Ramada is a reasonably priced hotel that allowed us to book the handicap room on the ground floor, so we could park our bikes in our room.

(65.8) Turn right on Market St. Go 0.1 mile.

(65.9) Turn left on San Fernando St. Go 0.7 mile.

(66.6) Turn right South 10th St. Go 0.5 mile.

(67.1) Turn left on East William St. Go 0.5 mile.

(67.6) Turn right into Selma Olinder Park. Go 0.5 mile following a section of the Coyote Creek Trail through the school and picnic areas then curve to the right and cross under the freeway.

Note: This trail is part the Coyote Creek Parkway, under the jurisdiction of Santa

through the weeds led us to the creek, but ended in a flooded homeless camp. Wet clothes lay in heaps and soggy sleeping bags were strewn everywhere, bits of river flotsam waved like flags on abandoned shopping carts.

We tried to push on and follow the creek further south but were blocked by poison oak and a chain link fence. Rather than turn back, or crawl through poison oak, we climbed the fence and found ourselves in a small neighborhood playground. We cut through the park then headed south again, following the creek on city streets, hoping to find a trail again. In a way we felt a little foolish for wasting so much time and effort looking for a "wild" route when it was pretty clear that the only thing we would find were homeless trails. But we had to try, it was the John Muir way to do things!

We followed a small road that led behind some small commercial buildings and came to the big open field of an old farm. Like in a John Muir nightmare, a big tractor with huge yellow jaws was flattening an old barn, smashing the old growth redwood planks to splinters. As we stood watching it wheeled around and grabbed an apple tree that had shaded the barn and tore it out by the roots. Muir had called the sheep that destroyed his beloved Sierra meadows the "hoofed locust". Today we have our own cause-of-blight, which I call the "steel locust." It is the speculators backhoe and tractor that destroys our history and old trees to make room for more new buildings and more business parks that we don't really need.

We finally made it to the Coyote Creek Trail again. Muir's winter of 1867-8 may have been the fourth rainiest, but according to records in the National Archives, our April was wetter than his April; we found the trail flooded by the swift moving water of Coyote Creek. Thinking yellow caution tape was for sissies, we ducked under it and started to wade across the creek, but the water was really deep and running too fast. We had to backtrack again. Consulting street maps we found a parallel path on little neighborhood streets. To reach them we had to cut cross-country through a field but ended up in a fenced horse stable so we had to backtrack a second time. Here is another irony: When John Muir took his thousand-mile walk he avoided trails to be in the wild places. Today trails are only found in the places set aside to experience nature and without them we would have no way to access the wild places.

Almaden to Coyote
(72.3 – 77.5)

The tree and brush-lined trail led us through silent wild places and I took special notice of Muir-esque things: poppies gleaming in a ray of sunlight, a big pile of tumbleweeds just ready to roll in the rising wind. I smelled sage; its usually grey leaves were bright green, bejeweled with purple puffball flowers. We passed huge valley

Clara County Parks. There are restrooms beyond the playgrounds near the ball field.

(68.1) Turn right and cross the abandoned train trestle bridge. Go 0.1 mile.

(68.2) Cross Story Rd. and follow Senter Rd. south. Go 1.6 miles.

Note: To the left is Kelley Park, with a zoo, ornamental gardens and the History Park. Historic buildings have been moved to the site and now display vintage artifacts. There are working trolleys, a print shop and exhibition galleries. This is a great place to get a sense of the history of the Silicon Valley. Open Tuesday through Sunday, noon to 5:00 pm. Free admission.

(69.8) Turn left on Tully Rd. Go 0.5 mile, passing the Tully Community Ballfields and Library on the right.

(70.3) Turn right on Kenoga Dr. Go 0.2 mile to its end at Sherlock Dr.

(70.5) Turn right and enter a neighborhood park. Go 1.3 miles following the path around a school, past play structures to a trailhead entrance for the Coyote Creek Bike Trail. Continue past the Los Lagos Golf Course.

(71.8) Turn right at a "T" junction and go under the Capitol Expressway to stay on the trail. Go 0.3 mile.

(72.1) The trail crosses to the west side of the creek. Go 0.2 mile.

(72.3) Turn left at a sign for the Coyote Creek Trail. Go 0.9 mile passing under Yerba Buena St. Follow the trail through Hellyer Park, passing west of the velodrome then passing restrooms with water on the left.

(73.2) When the trail forks stay right. Go 0.7 mile, continuing on the Coyote Creek Trail, skirting around Cottonwood Lake.

Note: Just west of the fork is a visitor center with a live rattlesnake. In the next few miles the trail passes by several magnificent old valley oaks.

(73.9) The trail passes under Highway 101. Go 0.7 mile.

(74.6) The trail crosses the creek on an old bridge. Go 1.6 miles.

(76.2) The trail passes under Silicon Valley Blvd. Go 0.7 mile.

Note: This is a good day's walk from downtown San Jose and the Holiday Inn San Jose-Silicon Valley is just steps from the trail. There is a good restaurant here too.

(76.9) The trail passes under Highways 101 and 85. Go 0.6 mile.

(77.5) Pass Metcalf Park, with restrooms on the right. Continue 0.9 mile, past Coyote Parkway Lake, then cross the creek on a covered bridge.

(78.4) Cross Metcalf Rd. turn left then right, following the signs for the Coyote Creek Trail. Go 0.8 mile.

(79.2) Turn left on Coyote Ranch Rd. Go 0.2 mile.

(79.4) Turn right at the "T" junction. Go 5.1 miles, crossing the creek several times as you continue on the Coyote Creek Bike Trail.

(84.5) Pass the Santa Clara Model Aircraft Skyport on the left. Go 1.6 miles.

oaks, twenty or thirty feet around and very old. The ground under the oaks was still almost dry. John Muir might have spent time waiting out storms under these very oaks. We ate our lunch under one.

Coyote to Morgan Hill (77.5 – 86.9)

The Coyote Valley is still very rural. The same beautiful views Muir recounted could still be seen from the trail. The rolling hills grew verdant emerald green, and orange poppies drooping in the rain dotted the fields. Cottonwoods and sycamores nestled in the creases of the hillsides, some of their leaves just beginning to unfurl bright green.

After about a mile the raging "creek" once again flooded the trail. We had two options: backtrack and take a 3 or 4 mile detour on roads to the west, or stay on the east side of the creek, cutting through empty fields to find the trail again past the flooded crossing. Overconfident of our route-finding skills we set out over the wet grassy hillside. After a mile or so our way was blocked by freeway, flooded creek and a thick forest of poison oak "trees". Backpacks and all we struggled to climb the freeway's 12 foot chain link fence then skirted around the poison oak on the freeway's wide grass shoulder. That was a big mistake. How would we explain to a highway patrol officer what we were doing next to the freeway? We didn't even notice climbing over the 12 foot fence we did it so fast.

Giant oaks near Morgan Hill

Morgan Hill to Jackson Ranch on East Dunne Road (86.9 – 93)

The rain had stopped. The sun was out. In the park above the Anderson Dam we found an isolated meadow with a small pond. We sat in the sunshine, reveling in the beauty. Turkey vultures and Canada geese flew in circles overhead and the frogs called to us. The hillsides shone and gleamed with a radiant brilliance only Muir's prose could properly describe. But it was a small park and we were soon back in civilization, walking through a residential neighborhood on roads that were not designed for walkers. There were no sidewalks. We had a good time studying the houses' varied architecture and landscaping, and then wondered if Muir would have enjoyed the sightseeing too, or if he would have thought of the subdivision just "wood, glass and concrete blight."

(86.1) The road forks at the Walnut Rest Area. Go 0.2 mile. Hikers follow the Sycamore Nature Trail right, cyclists stay left. These trails merge at a bridge.

(86.3) Cross the bridge. Go 0.5 mile.

(86.8) The Bike Trail ends at Eagle View Dr. Go one block south on Eagle View Dr.

(86.9) Turn left on Morning Star Dr. Go one block.

Note: This is the end of the recommended trip. We suggest you shuttle from here up to Henry Coe State Park, where the next recommended trip on the MRR begins, because East Dunne Rd. is 14 miles of twisting, narrow, dangerous, one and a half lane road. That said, we met a local cyclist, training for Olympic-type events, who rides it daily for exercise!

Directions for returning to the Fremont BART Station: Follow Malaguerra Ave. southeast 0.3 mile. Turn right on Cochrane Rd. Go 1.9 miles. Turn left on the Monterey Rd. Go 0.5 mile, passing under the railroad tracks. Turn right on Old Monterey Rd. Go 0.2 mile. Turn left on Llagas Rd. Go 0.2 mile to Hale Rd. The Valley Transit Authority VTA bus stop is at the northeast corner of the intersection. Take the #68 bus (it has bike racks on the front) north to the Diridon Transit Station in downtown San Jose.

Take the Express 180 bus to the Fremont BART Station and to your car. There are several places to eat along Cochrane Rd.

(87.0) Turn right on Malaguerra Ave. Go 0.5 mile.

(87.5) Turn left into Anderson County Park's oak shaded picnic area. Go 0.4 mile, following the Serpentine Trail beside the creek up to the Anderson Dam.

Note: Anderson County Park is part of the Santa Clara County Park system. It has hiking trails, picnic areas and provides access for both boating and fishing in the 1,250 acre Anderson Reservoir. Bikes are not allowed on trails in the park.

Note: Directions for bicycle route: Continue on Malaguerra. Go 0.5 mile. Turn left onto Cochrane Rd. Go 1.5 miles. Turn right on E. Main Ave. Go 0.3 mile. Turn left on Hill Rd. Go 1.1 miles. Turn left on East Dunne Rd. Go 0.8 mile. Connect with the MRR at mile 91.8.

(87.9) Turn right. Go 0.4 mile, crossing the dam and following the reservoir's edge to the boat launch area.

Note: The boat launch area has restrooms and water.

(88.3) Turn right. Go 1.4 miles, crossing the parking lot to the dirt road (Laguna Seca Trail) that leads up into the parklands. Follow the trail south and then east to a residential area called Holiday Lake Estates.

(89.7) Turn right on Holiday Dr. Go 2.1 miles following it through the subdivision.

We walked a few more hours up East Dunne Road, a narrow and twisted road also not made for walkers, to Jackson Ranch where we ended the day's walk. Waiting to be picked up by that evening's host, we rested against a giant old oak. It was wonderfully warm out, the gentle, sweet-smelling warm of sunshine after a long time of rain. We watched a male woodpecker do little loop-de-loops off the top of a power pole as he tried to get the attention of a female. A car drove by. The driver called out his window at us, "What a life!" Indeed...

Jackson Ranch to Henry Coe State Park Headquarters (93 – 101)

A friend had arranged special permission for us to walk through private ranch land from here to Henry Coe State Park. We left paved roads and civilization behind on a pastoral little dirt ranch road. It wound its way around small hills that were speckled with blue miniature lupines, yellow Johnny-jump-ups and little white popcorn flowers. The more distance we put between us and the "metal locust" of the city below, the better things got. We crossed a large fallow pasture, towards the ranch road that would take us to Henry Coe State Park. It was so full of yellow cream cups that Donna just had to stop and paint. I set out food and played my ukulele. The sun sent a few rays through the grey.

Journaling near Anderson Reservoir

(91.8) Turn left on East Dunne Rd.   Go 9.2 miles.

Note: This is a steep winding two-lane road with a narrow shoulder. Be extra careful. There is an outhouse on the east side of the reservoir at a fishing spot called Woodchoppers Flat.

(101.0) End at Henry Coe State Park's Coe Ranch Headquarters.

After lunch the trail really began to gain elevation. The steep hills were covered with the most magnificent old valley oaks, beautiful gnarled giants, probably hundreds of years old. Higher still we encountered thick fog and could not see more than fifty feet ahead. The great trees took on the appearance of giant ghosts. It began to rain again. We reached Henry Coe State Park's ridge-top campground just before dark, the vast panoramic views to the south lit flaming orange by the glow of sunset, and we finally felt as if we had found Muir's "anywhere that is wild".

Resources for Section One

Maps:
California State Auto
Association (AAA)
www.csaa.com

The Bay Trail Project
101 8th Street
Oakland, CA 94607
(510) 464-7900
www.baytrail.org

Transportation:
San Francisco Muni
11 South Van Ness Avenue
San Francisco, CA 94103
(415) 701-2311
www.sfmta.com

Alameda/Oakland Ferry
www.eastbayferry.com

BART
Bay Area Rapid Transit District
P.O. Box 12688
Oakland, CA 94604-2688
(510)465-2278
www.bart.gov

AC Transit
Oakland office:
1600 Franklin Street
(Oakland, CA 94612
(510)891-4706
www2.actransit.org

Yellow Cab Taxi Company
17551 Peak Ave.
Morgan Hill, CA 95037
(408)245-5222

Accommodations:
San Leandro Marina Inn
68 Monarch Bay Drive
San Leandro, CA 94577
(800) 786-7783
www.sanleandromarinainn.com

Marina Community Center
15301 Wicks Blvd.
San Leandro, CA 94579
(510) 577-6080
san-leandro.ca.us

Phoenix Lodge
2286 Industrial Pkwy W
Hayward, CA 94545
(510) 786-2844

Courtyard Newark Silicon
Valley
34905 Newark Blvd
Newark, CA 94560
(510) 792-5200
www.marriott.com/hotels

Good Nite Inn Fremont
4135 Cushing Parkway
Fremont, CA 94538
(510) 656-9307
www.goodnite.com/fremont

Ramada San Jose
455 South 2nd Street
San Jose, CA 95113
(408) 298-3500
ramada.com

Holiday Inn San Jose-
Silicon Valley
399 Silicon Valley Blvd.
San Jose, CA 95138
(877) 863-4780
ichotelsgroup.com

Organizations:

The Bay Trail Project
101 8th Street
Oakland, CA 94607
(510) 464-7900
www.baytrail.org

Laura Thompson (SF Bay Trail)
(510) 464-7935
laurat@abag.ca.gov

East Bay Regional Park
District Headquarters
2950 Peralta Oaks Court
PO Box 5381
Oakland, CA 94605
(510) 562-PARK
www.ebparks.org/parks/
hayward

Hayward Shoreline
Interpretive Center
3010 West Winton Ave.
Hayward, CA 94545
(510) 783-1066

Don Edwards San Francisco
Bay National Wildlife Refuge
9500 Thornton Ave.
Newark, CA 94560
(510) 792-0222
www.fws.gov/desfbay/
index.htm

Coyote Hills Regional Park
8000 Patterson Ranch Road
Fremont, CA 94555

Coyote Creek Trail
Guadalupe River Trail
www.sjparks.org/trails

History San Jose
1650 Senter Road.
San Jose, CA 95112
(408) 287-2290
www.historysanjose.org/
visiting_hsj/history_park/

Hellyer County Park
985 Hellyer Ave.
San Jose, CA 95111
(408) 225-0225
www.parkhere.org/portal/
site/parks/

Anderson Lake County Park
19245 Malaguerra Ave.
Morgan Hill, CA 95037
(408) 779-3634

Henry Coe State Park
9100 East Dunne Ave.
Morgan Hill, CA 95037
(408) 779-2728
www.coepark.org

Popcorn flowers near Poverty Flat, Henry Coe State Park

Section Two: Diablo Range

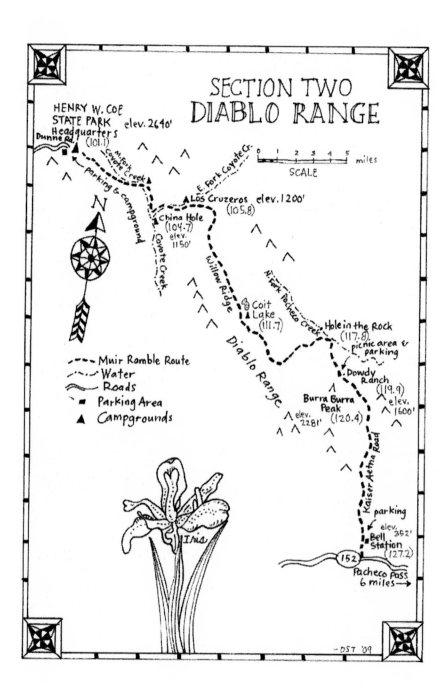

SECTION TWO
DIABLO RANGE

HENRY W. COE STATE PARK Headquarters elev. 2640' (101.1)
Dunne Rd.
M. Fork Coyote Creek
parking & campground
Coyote Creek
E. Fork Coyote Cr.

SCALE
0 1 2 3 4 5 miles

Los Cruzeros elev. 1200' (105.8)
China Hole (104.7) elev. 1150'

Willow Ridge

N. Fork Pacheco Creek

Coit Lake (111.7)

Diablo Range

Hole in the Rock (117.8)
picnic area & parking

Dowdy Ranch (119.9) elev. 1600'

Burra Burra Peak (120.4)
elev. 2281'

Kaiser Aetna Road

- - - Muir Ramble Route
Water
Roads
Parking Area
Campgrounds

parking
elev. 352'
Bell Station (127.2)

152
Pacheco Pass 6 miles →

Iris

- DST '09

Section Two: Diablo Range

Through Hike

Begin: Henry Coe State Park, Coe Ranch Headquarters
**End: Henry Coe State Park, Bell Station Entrance on
     Highway 152**
Distance: 26 miles

Section two of the MRR wanders through Henry W. Coe State Park (Coe) towards the Pacheco Pass. Coe is the largest State Park in Northern California, a vast wilderness situated just east of Morgan Hill and north of the Pacheco Pass. The terrain is rugged, varied and beautiful, with lofty ridges and steep canyons. From the park's one-lane dirt ranch roads and small trails you will see California much as it was when Muir walked by in 1868: a wilderness of rolling green hills covered with oaks and wildflowers, with ridge tops covered in dry chaparral. There are many trails, many routes to choose from, and with over 87,000 acres of wild open space you can hike for several weeks without backtracking. The MRR passes by places with picturesque names like Poverty Flat, the Narrows and Hole in the Rock. The route continues following the Kaiser Aetna Rd. past Dowdy Ranch, through pastoral rolling hills that have been neatly trimmed by grazing cattle, with continually changing panoramic views of the Pacheco Pass, San Joaquin Valley and Sierra Nevada to the south and east. The route ends at Coe's Bell Station entrance off of Highway 152.

Coe is at its best in the spring when water running in the creeks. The wildflowers will be blooming, and amazing both for the variety and quantity. Mountain bikes are allowed on trails in the park but we recommend this as a backpacking trip. Walking, "rambling" as Muir would call it, is the way to really see and appreciate the natural beauty of Henry Coe State Park.

Recommended Trip

Begin: Henry Coe State Park Coe Ranch Headquarters
**End: Henry Coe State Park Bell Station Entrance on
     Highway 152**
Distance: 26 miles

The Recommended Trip follows the MRR through this section from beginning to end. We suggest taking it as a four-day backpack trip, but it could be done in three days by starting early and spending the first night at Coit Lake. Remember backpacking miles can be long and hard (but enjoyable and rewarding) so don't plan to travel as many in a day as you would in a more urban section. One good way to do this trip is with two shuttle cars. First, leave one in the small Henry Coe Bell Station parking lot (put a note in the window for the rangers that you are on a backpack trip) then drive to the Park Ranch Headquarters on Dunne Rd. to start your trip.

We suggest you leave plenty of time to get started and only plan to make Day One a half-day. It is a steep 5-mile hike from the Coe Ranch Headquarters trailhead at an elevation of 2,644 feet to the Los Cruzeros campsite at 1,220 feet. You will have great panoramic views as the MRR follows trails and ranch roads past steep wooded hillsides and vast fields of flowers. There is a swimming hole near the halfway point. Day Two is a 7-mile hike that climbs from the creek on a single-track trail then follows the ridge line passing Coit Lake at an elevation of 2,099 feet where there are several nice camp sites. Day Three is also a 7-mile hike. First the route stays high, climbing up and down ridge tops. Then it follows a faint steep trail down to the North Fork Pacheco Creek to a campsite near a nice swimming spot called Hole in the Rock at an elevation of 833 feet. Day four is a half-day 8.3-mile hike on dirt road that starts with a mile-long 1,600 foot climb and finishes with a 7.3-mile descent to Highway 152. Even though this is more miles than other days it should only take a half-day because it is mostly downhill.

What you need and need to know

Maps:

Street Maps: AAA Sectional Series Central California

Park Maps: Henry Coe State Park. This is a very good topographical map available at the Headquarters. It can also be ordered in advance from the Pine Ridge Association.

Accommodations:

Camping is allowed in Henry Coe State Park.

Register:

Before you leave on your hike register at the Park Head-quarters. Ask for updates on trail conditions and recommendations for places to camp. If there is no one at the Visitor Center, self-register, pay the fee to park your car (there are parking spaces beside a big barn to the southeast of the Center), and leave a note that describes your planned route. If you are shuttling be sure to let them know your second car is parked at the Bell Station parking lot.

Water:

In spring you will be able to find water in the streams, springs, and lakes on the MRR. The water will need to be purified before drinking. In summer and fall the streams and springs may be dry. Check with the ranger before leaving.

Poison Oak:

Poison oak arches over many of the smaller trails. If you don't know what it looks like, ask at the visitor center.

A Word of Warning:

The terrain is rugged and the weather can be severe, so be prepared! On the first day the trail passes through The Narrows. If it has been raining check to see if this section is passable, or whether you will need to use an alternate trail to get to Los Cruzeros.

Section Two Trailhead Information

Through Hike Beginning Trailhead:

Access by Car: Exit Highway 101 on East Dunne Rd. Go east for 12 miles, to the end of the road at the Coe Ranch Head-quarters. Access by Public Transportation: Yellow Cab Taxi Co.

Ending Trailhead:

Access by Car: Turn north off Highway 152 (6.9 miles east of the junction of Highway 152 and 156) on the Kaiser Aetna Rd. From the highway the Kaiser Aetna Rd. looks like a little driveway just to the west of the deserted Bell Station Restaurant. Access by Public Transportation: Yellow Cab Taxi Co.

Recommend Trip Beginning Trailhead:

Same as above.

Henry Coe State Park's campground is nestled around old farm buildings left from the original Coe Ranch. We were scheduled to give a presentation about our adventure late in the afternoon. It rained and poured again so we spent much of the day standing by a wood stove in the visitor's center. There weren't many visitors because of the weather, but with family, friends and the park's Pine Ridge Association volunteers in attendance, our talk became a quite festive occasion as we rolled out our twenty-foot long map of Alameda and Santa Clara counties and described where we had walked and what had happened so far.

It was a Muir miracle that the rain let up just as we finished talking, so everyone joined us on a short steep hike to Frog Lake. The trail was festooned with shooting star and hound's tongue in full bloom, harbingers of what was to come. We reached a promontory with a vast view of the park. As Donna studied the landscape with our friend George Koenig, he said, "You guys are so lucky. This is going to be the trip of your life. It's going to be loud out there, so loud you are going to hear the sounds of the flowers blooming and the grass growing."

"What does that sound like?" I asked.

"You'll know when you hear it!"

Section Two Directions

(101.0) Begin by following the Corral Trail, which leaves just across the street from the Coe Ranch Headquarters. Go 0.6 mile. You will immediately experience the magic of the park as this trail winds in and out of oak forests and wildflower meadows.

(101.6) Just after the intersection with Forest Trail and Springs Trail you will reach Manzanita Point Rd. Once on the road, continue straight ahead, heading southeast. Go 0.9 mile, down a wide-open rolling hillside, past several walk-in campsites.

(102.5) Turn left on the Poverty Flat Rd. Go 1.6 miles.

Note: Poverty Flat Rd. is shin-splintingly steep, but passes some amazingly beautiful giant red-trunk manzanita and hillsides of shooting stars. If you desire a less steep route, follow this alternate route: Continue 0.4 mile on Manzanita Point Rd. Turn left on the China Hole Trail. Go 1.1 miles. Stay right at the junction with Cougar Trail. Go 1.6 miles continuing on the China Hole Trail. Turn left at China Hole, a nice deep swimming spot on the Middle Fork of the Coyote Creek, that is worth a detour if you want to swim. Go 0.1 mile up stream to the East Fork of the Coyote Creek to rejoin the MRR at mile 104.7.

(104.1) The road crosses the Middle Fork of the Coyote Creek. Go 0.1 mile past shaded campsites and a restroom.

(104.2) Just past campsite #5, turn right at a trail sign for China Hole.

Go 0.5 mile, following a creekside trail downstream.

(104.7) Turn left at the first tributary, which is the East Fork Coyote Creek. Go 1.1 miles upstream.

Note: Start by following the north bank. The trail will crisscross the creek through "The Narrows", passing clear little pools and sculpted rock pinnacles. The river valley will then widen out with open grasslands on both sides.

The Narrows in Henry Coe State Park

(105.8) Continue past a big clearing called Los Cruzeros. Go 0.2 mile staying on the east side of the creek.

Note: Los Cruzeros is a good half-day hike from the trailhead and a good place to camp. It has three large campsites, and upstream there are a few small pools in the creek to dip in.

(106.0) Cross Poverty Flat Rd. Continue east for a few feet on the trail. At the next trail junction turn right on Willow Ridge Trail. Go 1.6 miles following this steep single-track trail up the hill.

Note: There can be a profusion of flowers on this trail in springtime. In 1.3 miles you will pass No Name Trail on the right. It leads to a trickling water source called Willow Ridge Spring and just beyond that there is a beautiful dry campsite under giant oaks, with a stunning view into Kelly Cabin Canyon.

(107.6) Turn right on Willow Ridge Rd.

**Poverty Flat to Coit Lake
(104.1 – 111.7)**

We stopped for lunch at Los Cruzeros, a camp site that is a day and a half from the Coe Ranch Headquarters. We hadn't seen anyone since we left and we felt a million miles from anywhere. We decided to wash off in the creek and had just started to strip when out of nowhere came five guys, flying down the trail on mountain bikes. It must be a law of nature: whenever you bare your butt someone will appear, no matter how long it has been since you saw the last person. They stopped to chat for a few moments: "Where have you been? Where are you going? Did you see the goldfields in bloom?" The wilderness seemed to make them especially friendly. Cyclists never stopped to chat when we were hiking the biking trails in the city.

As soon as they left we completed our skinny-dip in the

93

creek and then rested. Donna painted. I wrote some, played my uke, then closed my eyes and listened to the sounds of the water. I began to stare at the clouds and thought about how I rarely stop to notice nature when I am at home. I could say that nature is hard to find in a city, but that would only be an excuse. The fact is that I just don't take the time. Then I remembered what George said, "It's going to be loud out there." I shifted my focus from the river to the plants. The first thing I heard was an airplane overhead but after that I think maybe I did hear the plants growing.

Coit Lake to Dowdy Ranch (111.7 – 120.4)

We camped in a meadow by Coit Lake and woke to find our tent in a sea of sparkling white frost. We walked to the lake and pumped drinking water. Even filtered, it tasted like algae. That made us wonder if John Muir drank tea just to mask the bad taste or if he knew that boiling his water would kill the bacteria.

We hiked hard all day over the sharp ridges and deep canyons of Coe Park and in the end reached a high point of the Diablo Range where the world dropped off in all directions and we had a 360-degree view: distant mountains framed by a cloudless blue sky above us, below rolling hills were speckled with oaks and pines and dotted with little patches of color from millions of wildflowers in distant meadows. There was no trace of

Go 3.5 miles following the crest of the ridge towards Coit Lake.

Note: There are beautiful views in all directions. If you need to cool off, in 1.6 miles there is trail to the left for Hoover Lake. It is not much to look at, but wet, and only ten minutes off the trail.

(111.1) Continue past a road with a trail sign for Coit Dam. Go 0.6 mile.

(111.7) Coit Rd. splits to the left. Willow Ridge Rd. becomes Crest Trail. Continue straight ahead on Crest Trail. Go 1 mile.

Note: It is a good day's hike from Los Cruzeros to Coit Lake. If you want to spend the night at Coit Lake turn left here. Go 0.3 mile and you will reach the south end of Coit Lake. Follow the road to the left, staying on the west side of the lake, and go 0.2 mile. You will come to a nice improved campsite with a restroom. If that site is occupied, a faint trail around the southeast end of the lake will take you to the horse camp. It is unimproved but has a metal corral on a flower-garden hillside and great views of the lake. Below the campsite the lake seems inaccessible but we found it wasn't. We just had to slide over 10 feet of reeds to get to the water for a swim!

(112.7) Pass the Kelly Lake Trail on the right. Go 0.2 mile.

Note: In 0.1 mile you will reach the highest point of the trip passing by an unnamed peak at an elevation of 2625 feet, with a 360-degree view of the park and beyond.

(112.9) Turn right on Wagon Rd. and go 0.8 very steep mile.

(113.7) Turn left at the next trail junction, which is the inappropriately named Center Flats Rd. Go 2.4 miles, rising and falling over a series of steep hills.

(116.1) Pass Walsh Trail on the left. Go 0.2 mile.

(116.3) Turn left on Scherrer Trail. Go 0.7 mile descending as the trail follows a series of little sloping ridges.

Note: Scherrer Trail is a cutoff to the Kaiser Aetna Rd., which leads to a swimming spot called "Hole in the Rock" on the North Fork of Pacheco Creek. The trail is easy to miss. No signs are posted and only a faint old trail leaves Center Flats Rd. and heads down the hill. This trail will get so faint you will think you have lost it, but look for a cut in a hillside or a swath of goldfields through the grass to show you the way. It is a lightly used trail, a real adventure to follow, but even if you lose it you can just keep going downhill and you will eventually get to Kaiser Aetna Rd. If you want to avoid the cross-country hiking, extra miles and 1600 feet of elevation change, follow this alternate route:

Continue on Center Flats Rd. Go 1.5 miles. Turn right on the Hersman Pond Trail. Go 0.4 mile. Meet with the MRR at mile 119.7

(117.2) Stay left, and head downhill. Go 0.3 mile.

Note: The right fork goes up hill to man-made Scherrer Pond.

(117.5) Turn left on Kaiser Aetna Rd. Go 0.3 mile.

Note: This road is occasionally used by ranchers and they won't be expecting hikers, so watch out for fast moving

humans anywhere. There were no reservoirs or aqueducts, no giant electric towers with wires stretching across the landscape, and no super highway winding its way down to new housing sprawl in the San Joaquin Valley. It was the same awe-inspiring panorama Muir had described from the Pacheco Pass in 1868: "for there, in clear view, over heaps and rows of foothills, is laid a grand, smooth, outspread plain, watered by a river, and another range of peaky, snow-capped mountains a hundred miles in the distance. That plain is the valley of the San Joaquin, and those mountains are the great Sierra Nevada." And we were seeing it from Henry Coe State Park in 2006.

Dowdy Ranch to Bell Station: (120.4 - 127.2)

We hopped out of bed just before daylight, two crazy John Muirs, bent on seeing the "Range of Light" at sunrise. Hints of daylight already tinged the dark sky with color. We sprinted the last 50 vertical feet to miraculously make it in time. There, beyond the Diablos, like a ghost in the distance, were the peaks of the Sierra backlit by the rising sun. It was a magic moment in a magic place and we couldn't help ourselves: we whooped and howled like coyotes.

With no rain clouds in sight and the temperature 75-80, it was like the first day of spring. Donna kept saying, "Listen to the birds sing. They are as excited as we are to have the sun." We spent most of the day lollygagging in the sunshine, meandering down the Kaiser-Aetna Road to Bell Station. Ungrazed pastureland bordered both sides of the road. Orange fiddlenecks stretched their heads above the green grass as if trying to get a better look at the odd two-legged visitors. A golden eagle soared overhead, too high for us to see clearly, even with binoculars. As it dropped lower, two small crows attacked it and tried to scare it away from either a nest or some young birds. Were the crows being valiant or crazy? We couldn't decide.

Near the bottom of the Kaiser-Aetna Road a young steer appeared on the road ahead. He had clearly escaped his pasture and was sufficiently frightened by us that he ran every time we got near. Try as we might, we couldn't get around him to chase him back up the road and he stayed ahead of us all the way to Bell Station. Unfortunately the gate at Highway 152 had an opening for bicycles that was also just big enough for a cow, and he raced through it, straight for the busy highway. We were going to be in big trouble. Muir luck struck again. An obviously concerned driver who clearly had no more experience chasing loose cattle than we had drove towards it honking his horn, trying to get it off the road. Between the three of us, Donna and I frantically running, waving our arms and whooping, we rounded up that little doggie and got it headed back up the dirt road towards home.

trucks.

(117.8) Turn left on an unmarked trail that follows the North Fork of the Pacheco Creek upstream. Go 0.1 mile and you will find Hole in the Rock.

Note: This is a good days hike from Coit Lake and a great place to spend a night. There is a big swimming hole with a little waterfall. There are campsites on the grassy bench just upstream of the pool or downstream on the other side of the road.

(117.9) Return to Kaiser Aetna Rd. and turn right. Go 1.8 miles, past the Scherrer Trail, and up a steep 20% grade.

(119.7) Pass Hersman Pond Trail on the right. Go 0.2 mile.

(119.9) Pass Dowdy Ranch on the left. Go 0.5 mile.

Note: Dowdy Ranch, with water, restrooms, picnic areas, horse corrals and a visitor center, is open seasonally, on weekends and holidays, from 8:00 am to sunset. Vehicle access is allowed on a limited basis. Check with the Henry Coe Park Headquarters Visitor Center for current information. A day use fee is charged.

(120.4) Pass the trail to Burra Burra Peak on the right. Kaiser Aetna Rd. curves left. Go 6.8 miles down the nicely graded dirt road, winding through pastoral rolling hills, neatly trimmed by cattle grazing, with continually changing panoramic views to the south and east.

Note: If it is a clear day, in the distance to the east you will be able to see the Sierra Nevada, gleaming over mountain ridges of the Pacheco Pass. Muir was slightly south of here when he described it as the "Range of Light", but this spot is very close both in location and in spirit. The landscape seems mostly unchanged from what Muir described when he walked by in 1868.

(127.2) End at Highway 152.

Note: There is a parking area here, and camping at Casa de Fruta 6 miles to the west, or by reservation at Pacheco State Park 6 miles to the east.

Walking towards the Pacheco Pass on the Kaiser Aetna Road

Resources for Section Two

Maps:

Pine Ridge Association
Map Request
9100 East Dunne Ave
Morgan Hill, CA 95037
(408) 782-9241
www.coepark.org/map-intro.html

Transportation:

Yellow Cab Taxi Company
17551 Peak Ave.
Morgan Hill, CA 95037
(408) 245-5222
www.yellowcabca.com

Accommodations:

Casa De Fruta
10031 Pacheco Pass Hwy
Hollister, CA 95023
(831) 637-2666
www.casadefruta.com

Pacheco State Park
Park Headquarters
38787 Dinosaur Point Road
Hollister, CA 95023
(209) 826-6283
www.parks.ca.gov/?page_id=560

Henry Coe State Park
9100 East Dunne Ave.
Morgan Hill, CA 95037
(408) 779-2728
www.coepark.org

Looking west near Dowdy Ranch, Henry Coe State Park

Pacheco State Park

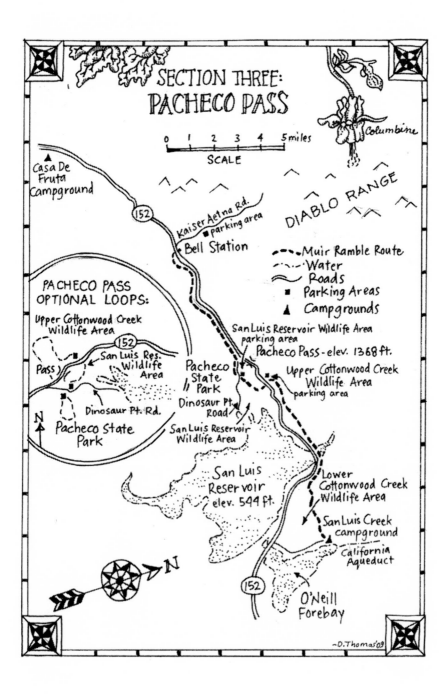

SECTION THREE:
PACHECO PASS

Columbine

0 1 2 3 4 5 miles
SCALE

Casa De Fruta Campground

152

DIABLO RANGE

Kaiser Aetna Rd.
■ parking area
Bell Station

‑‑‑‑ Muir Ramble Route
‑‑‑‑ Water
‑‑‑‑ Roads
■ Parking Areas
▲ Campgrounds

PACHECO PASS
OPTIONAL LOOPS:

Upper Cottonwood Creek
Wildlife Area

152

San Luis Res.
Wildlife Area

Pass)

San Luis Reservoir Wildlife Area
parking area
Pacheco Pass - elev. 1368 ft.

Pacheco
State
Park

Upper Cottonwood Creek
Wildlife Area
parking area

Dinosaur Pt. Rd.

Dinosaur Pt.
Road

N

San Luis Reservoir
Wildlife Area

Pacheco State
Park

San Luis
Reservoir
elev. 544 ft.

Lower
Cottonwood Creek
Wildlife Area

San Luis Creek
campground

California
Aqueduct

N

152

O'Neill
Forebay

~D.Thomas'09

Section Three: Pacheco Pass

Through Hike

> **Begin: Henry Coe State Park Bell Station Entrance, Highway 152**
>
> **End: San Luis Creek Recreation Area Campground, O'Neill Forebay**
>
> **Distance: 20.8 miles**

Section Three of the MRR crosses the Diablo Range over the Pacheco Pass. It begins with no alternative but to follow Highway 152 to get up to the pass. This is a highway, not a freeway so technically pedestrians are allowed, but it is a very busy and dangerous four-lane road. We searched for alternatives but there are none: the land on both sides of the highway is private. Perhaps some day there will be a pedestrian right-of-way using the fire roads that run beside the highway, but today the only safe way to get to the pass is by car.

From the pass the MRR heads down the eastern side of the Diablo Range following firebreaks and ranch roads through the San Luis Reservoir, Upper Cottonwood Creek and Lower Cottonwood Creek Wildlife Areas. These wildlife areas are managed by the California Department of Fish and Game and are primarily used during hunting season (autumn and winter). They are practically unused the rest of the year. Of all the places we have hiked, this is where we found it easiest to imagine we were still in Muir's 1868 California. In springtime there are literally seas of flowers.

Keep your eyes open for tule elk. They are larger than deer, have a prominent white rump and travel in herds: a bull with up to thirty females and calves. It is estimated that before the gold rush there were half a million tule elk roaming the grasslands from the Sierra Nevada foothills to the coast. By Muir's day they were nearly gone, but were saved from extinction by cattleman Henry Miller who then owned millions of acres of land in California and Oregon including much of the land around Pacheco Pass. Today it is estimated there are over 2,000 tule elk in herds found on 22 reserves between Tomales Bay and Bakersfield.

The section ends at the edge of the O'Neill Forebay. This man-made body of water is part of the San Luis Reservoir State Recreation Area and is used for boating, fishing and camping. The water comes from Sierra Nevada snowmelt.

Recommended Trip

Begin: San Luis Reservoir Wildlife Area parking lot. (MRR mile 133.7)

End: San Luis Creek Recreation Area Campground. O'Neill Forebay. (MRR mile 148)

Distance: 14.3 miles

The recommended trip is a 14.3 miles hike from the top of the pass to the O'Neill Forebay, rambling through wildlife preserves. The terrain is rough. The trails are often firebreaks that have been graded without hikers in mind. Overnight camping is not allowed, so the trip has to be done as a day hike. It will be a long and hard day but it will have its rewards. There will be incredible opportunities to see wildflowers and wildlife, you will probably not see another person all day and many places will feel as if they have not changed since Muir walked through!

The trip begins by going up and down the ranch roads of the San Luis Reservoir Wildlife Area. The route then crosses Highway 152 and continues into the Lower Cottonwood Creek Wildlife Area. From MRR mile 141.2 to mile 142.6 there is no alterative but to walk on the wide shoulder of Highway 152. Walking beside a busy highway is dangerous. If you attempt this, take all the proper precautions including traveling in good daylight, walking against traffic, wearing fluorescent clothing and staying as far from traffic as possible. The route ends at the San Luis Creek Recreation Area Campground on the O'Neill Forebay.

Alternate Recommended Trips

We recommend two different day hikes loops from the top of the pass that can be taken as alternatives to the challenging recommended trip. Both leave from MRR mile 133.7, and both will give you access to this relatively unknown beautiful oak grassland area.

Alternate Recommended Trip One

This is a very strenuous 13 miles loop-hike that first follows the MRR through the San Luis Wildlife Area to the parking area at MRR mile 137.6, then loops back through the remote sections of the Upper Cottonwood Creek Wildlife Area. This wildlife area is incredibly beautiful with miles of open oak grasslands and views of rolling hills in all directions. From one point you can see Mt. Hamilton to the northwest, Fremont Peak to the southwest, the San Luis Reservoir to the south and on a clear day, the Sierra Nevada to the east. It is also extraordinarily under-utilized and one of the places where it seemed John Muir's footprints were still fresh. Alternatively the first part of this trip can be done as a 6.5 miles one-way trip to the Upper Cottonwood Creek Wildlife Parking Area if you have a shuttle vehicle.

Alternate Recommended Trip Two

This is an easy 4.5 miles loop trip in Pacheco State Park. Access to the park is directly across Dinosaur Point Rd. from the San Luis Reservoir Wildlife Area parking lot at MRR mile 133.6. This hike will take you on pastoral little roads into the area where the 1868 road over the Pacheco Pass was located. When we have hiked there we have been completely alone, and in spring the poppies have been like orange blankets on the rolling hills.

What you need and need to know

Maps:

Street Maps: AAA California Regional Series maps: Gold Country, Monterey Bay.

Compass Maps: Merced County

Merced Park Maps: San Luis Creek Wildlife Area and Upper and Lower Cottonwood Creek Wildlife Area maps are found at the registration kiosks in each area's parking lot or can be obtained ahead of time from the Fish and Game office.

Topographical Maps: USGS 7.5 minute: Pacheco Pass Quadrangle, San Luis Dam Quadrangle.

Accommodations:

There is camping at the San Luis Creek Recreation Area

Campground by the O'Neill Forebay. You can camp at Pacheco State Park, but this must be arranged in advance with the Park's Ranger. Camping is not allowed in the Upper and Lower Cottonwood Creek Wildlife Areas, except in the parking lots.

Self-Register:

Before leaving the parking areas, self-register at the wooden kiosk in the Wildlife Area parking lot.

Restrooms and Water:

There are restrooms at both trailheads. There is no water at the beginning trailhead, but there is non-potable water in Pacheco State Park. There may be water in springs or streams along the route.

WARNING

Hiking this section of the MRR can involve crossing or walking beside Highway 152. Be extremely careful. We recommend wearing florescent vests when on the highway.

The landscape is steep and the hiking is strenuous. There is very little shade and it can be very hot in the spring, summer and fall.

Deer hunting season generally begins the third Sunday in September and goes through October. Take extra caution if you hike during hunting season.

No open fires are permitted anywhere.

Section Three Trailhead Information

Through Hike Beginning Trailhead:

Access by Car: Turn north off Highway 152 (6.9 miles east of the junction of Highway 152 and 156) on Kaiser Aetna Rd.

Access by Public Transportation: none

Ending Trailhead:

Access by Car: The entrance for the San Luis Creek Recreation Area is near the bottom of the pass, about 6 miles west of Highway 5, and 10 miles east of Dinosaur Point Rd. Turn east and follow the entrance road. Go 0.4 mile to an entrance kiosk. (Currently $6 for day use or $25 for overnight camping.) Go 0.5

mile. Turn left at the sign for San Luis Creek Camping. Go 2.1 miles to the campground and day use parking area.

Note: We suggest you pay for overnight camping and leave your car in the campground. Talk to the camp host to arrange where to park.

Access by Public Transportation: none

Recommended Trip Beginning Trailhead:

Access by Car: From Highway 152, just west of the pass, turn south on Dinosaur Point Rd. Follow the sign for Pacheco Pass State Park. Go 0.5 mile. Turn left into the San Luis Reservoir Wildlife Area parking lot with free parking, or turn right to park at the Pacheco Pass State Park with a day use fee. If you are leaving your car overnight we recommend you park in Pacheco State Park and pay for overnight camping.

Access by Public Transportation: None

Ending Trailhead:

Same as above.

Alternate Trip One Beginning Trailhead:

The same as for the Recommended Trip.

Ending Trailhead:

Access by Car: The Upper Cottonwood Creek Wildlife Area parking lot is on the north side of Highway 152 about 2.5 miles east or down the grade from Dinosaur Point Rd. You can also start Alternate Recommended Trip One here and cut off 3.8 miles, making it a more manageable one day hike. Take the normal precautions required when leaving a car in an unattended parking area.

Alternate Trip Two Trailhead:

This trip begins and ends at the Recommended Trip Beginning Trailhead.

Even before Muir walked past here, Bell Station was a place to find a drink. In 1864 William Brewer called it Hollenbeck's Tavern and reported that he ate supper, talked in the barroom on Succession, then spent the night wishing he had his blankets to sleep outside, as the tavern's fleas "crawled over me in active troops." Like Brewer, and Muir, we would have enjoyed a meal and a beer, but the old restaurant has been vacant for years. That is a big difference between walking in California today and in 1868. In Muir's day there was a place to stay and eat every 15 miles along the existing travel routes. Today food and lodging can only be found where cars go and not in places people can safely walk.

When first planning our trip in Muir's footsteps we almost gave up at Bell Station. In Muir's day, a small dirt road wound its way east from Bell Station. Today, the only way to get over the pass is Highway 152. We spent months contacting local ranchers but we never could get permission to walk using the firebreaks beside the highway. It took awhile, but finally we realized that Highway 152 is a highway and not a freeway, so legal to walk on. Not safe, but legal.

Lucky the highway has a wide shoulder. Alex McInturff, a 23-year-old earth sciences student at Stanford, was the first person to follow the MRR route

Section Three Directions

(127.2) Turn left (east) on Highway 152. Go 5.9 miles.

(133.1) Turn right on Dinosaur Point Rd., a small paved road just past the truck pull-out before the top of the pass. Go 0.5 mile.

(133.6) Turn left into the San Luis Reservoir Wildlife Area parking lot. Go 0.1 mile crossing the parking lot.

Note: The recommended trip starts here, as do the Alternate Recommended Trips. There is an outhouse in the parking lot, and there are outhouses and water at the State Park across the road.

Directions for Alternate Recommended Trip One:

Begin at the San Luis Wildlife Area parking lot on Dinosaur Point Rd. Follow the MRR from mile 133.6 to mile 137.8. After you have passed through the gate of the second parking lot for the Upper Cottonwood Creek Wildlife Area turn left and head up the steep dirt road. Follow it along the ridgeline for a few miles heading towards the north boundary of the wildlife area. At the boundary veer left, following the road for a couple more miles west, dropping down to a spring and then back up. When you reach a substantial north-south running ranch road (Fifield Rd.) you have hit the western boundary. Turn left and follow Fifield downhill as it runs in and out of the Area's western boundary (at times you will need to walk parallel trails in the Wildlife Area). In about 2 miles you will near Highway 152. Follow the corral fence west to Fifield Rd. Carefully cross the highway and walk east on Dinosaur Point Rd. back to the parking area.

Directions for Alternate Recommended Trip Two:

Enter the Pacheco Pass State Park. There is a $5 day use fee. The trailhead gate is to the southwest of the parking lot. Maps can be found online and sometimes are in the kiosk at the trailhead. Follow Spikes Peak Trail to Up & Over to Canyon Loop West to Pig Pond Trail, a 4.5 mile round trip.

(133.7) Follow the dirt road that is northeast of the self-registration kiosk. Go 0.2 mile, eastward up the hill.

(133.9) Pass a USGS benchmark for Pacheco Pass on the left side of the road. Go 0.6 mile.

Note: From here you can see Highway 152 going over the pass. To the east you can see the vast expanse of the San Luis Reservoir, and in the distance, on a clear day, the flat San Joaquin Valley and perhaps even the Sierra Nevada.

(134.5) Turn left at the next junction. Go 0.1 mile, heading north.

(134.6) Pass a road on the right. Go 0.2 mile, continuing forward, going down the hill.

(134.8) Turn right at the next junction. The road levels out a bit here. Go 0.3 mile.

(135.1) Pass a road on the right. Continue straight ahead on a very steep descent down the hill. Go 0.8 mile, passing a small pond on the left.

Note: Ponds like this were built to water the cattle that grazed these former ranchlands.

over the *Pacheco Pass*: "When you walk in John Muir's footsteps, it's not supposed to be like this. 'Every car that passes you has a different sound, and you wonder which one will be the death knell...'"[2]

It is so discouraging: the fact that cars have been given first priority when it comes to transportation in California. Is it too much to ask for pedestrians and cyclists to have safe and pleasant access through the lands that we collectively own, these roads where now only a car travels safely? We vowed to let our representatives in government know that we want the needs of walkers and cyclists to be considered when this highway over *Pacheco Pass* gets repaired or improved. It would be another way to follow Muir's footsteps.

Pacheco State Park
(133.7)

We camped the night at the top of the pass in the *Pacheco State Park*. The next day we set out to find the actual road Muir had followed over the pass. The rangers told us there were remnants of it just east of the park boundary. We left the campground following a meandering dirt road lined by an old wooden fence, each fence pole crowned by a chirping bird that announced our coming and encouraged us onward. The grass covering these rolling Diablo Range hills was gleaming a blinding green, wildflowers shone in the sun, and to top it off, we had the

Upper Cottonwood Creek Wildlife Area

(135.9) Cross the creek at the bottom of the canyon. Go 100 feet.

(135.9) Turn left at the junction, then turn right up a very steep firebreak. Go 0.3 mile.

(136.2) Continue straight through a 4-way intersection at the top of the hill. Go 0.7 mile eastwards, down the hill towards the reservoir. Cross the bottom of the next canyon at the reservoir level, then continue uphill again.

(136.9) Pass a road on the right. Go 0.4 mile.

(137.3) Turn right at the next junction. Go 0.1 mile down the hill to a gate.

(137.4) Climb the gate. Go 0.1 mile up a paved roadway to a turnout on Highway 152.

Note of Warning: Be very careful crossing Highway 152. Remember the cars are going over 70 MPH! They move quicker than you will imagine and aren't used to seeing pedestrians here. It is a busy road, so WAIT for a BIG gap between the cars. It will come. This is also a place to leave a shuttle vehicle.

(137.5) Cross the highway. Go 0.1 mile, down a small road to the Upper Cottonwood Creek Wildlife Area parking lot.

(137.6) Pass around a green gate on the left side of the parking lot. Go 0.1 mile on a dirt road.

(137.7) Cross another parking lot and pass around another green gate. Continue straight ahead. Go 0.1 mile.

(137.8) Turn right on a big road/firebreak. Go 0.3 miles to the creek.

(138.1) Cross the creek and turn right on trail leading towards the highway. Go 0.1 mile.

(138.2) Stay left at the fork. Go 0.3 mile uphill.

(138.5) At the next junction, stay right. Go 0.5 mile as the road dips down towards the highway, passes a spring on the left and then heads up hill again.

(139.0) At the top of the ridge pass a road on the left. Go 0.3 mile down the hill.

(139.3) Pass Upper East Reservoir in the bottom of the canyon. Go 0.3 mile heading up the hill.

(139.6) Pass a spring. Go 0.3 mile.

(139.9) Turn right at the junction, heading down the hill. Go 1.2 miles.

Note: From here there are great views of the reservoir and to the east beyond.

(141.1) Turn right at the bottom of the drainage. Go 0.1 mile, over two gates, up to a turnout on Highway 152.

Warning: We do not recommend walking on the highway shoulder if you feel at all uncomfortable with the idea. Instead, we suggest you shuttle the next 1.4 miles in a car. We found it best to stay on the north side of the road so we could walk facing traffic, and we wore florescent vests!

whole place to ourselves. The highway was less than a quarter mile to the north but we felt far away from civilization. Even though we could not find the traces of the Pacheco Pass Road we were not disappointed, it was beautiful, and so Muir-like.

After returning to camp for supplies we took a second very long loop hike through hunting lands that border the park and highway to the north and east. The trails for the most part were really firebreaks, cut at an unimaginably knee-banging steep grade. But the vast unobstructed views were a commensurate reward. At one point we could see Mt. Hamilton to the north, Fremont Peak to the west, the reservoir to the south and a haze that was the Sierra to the east. The landscape was an oak-dotted grassland, some of the grass was still green, but most was already dying, giving the opposite hills a soft straw color. Again we could imagine Muir beside us: this was still like the California he saw in 1868. Again we were alone, no trace of humans, except their trash. We filled a backpack with hunters' empty water bottles.

Pacheco State Park to O'Neill Forebay (133.7 - 148)

The trip from the pass to the forebay was tough. We sweated up and down the steep firebreak roads, complaining a bit, not feeling at all like the mythical indefatigable John Muir who would have been reveling in the challenge. But even though we were grumbling, we were happy to be there: when we had driven in this area planning our trip we assumed it was all private ranch land and could not figure out what to do. It took two years of reconnaissance before we found legal access, following the firebreaks as roads through the three contiguous wildlife areas in this seemingly inaccessible, inhospitable mountainous region.

It was worth the pain. It was an amazingly clear day and there were vast views into the San Joaquin Valley with the Sierra Nevada looming in the distance. We drank them in whenever we took a breather from the straight up and down hiking. Coming over a rise we startled a herd of tule elk, deer-like animals with protruding chests and proud white rumps. Maybe it would be more accurate to say they startled us when they stampeded down the ravine. Over the next rise we crossed an old roadbed. It was the road over Pacheco Pass we had been looking for yesterday. We got down on hands and knees and searched for traces of Muir's footprints.

We dodged racing semis to cross Highway 152 and get into the Upper Cottonwood Creek Wildlife Area. After that we stopped complaining about the firebreaks: they were way better than the alternative, which was walking on the highway. Halfway down the grade we did have to walk beside the highway for about a mile as the

(141.2) Turn left. Go 0.7 mile following the highway east then south.

(141.9) Cross the reservoir. Continue 0.7 mile, passing a large private property sign, for the Romero Ranch, posted on the fence to the left. Continue until you come to a fisherman's parking area on the reservoir side of the road.

Note: If you want to take this as a two-day hike, this parking area is one place to leave a shuttle vehicle. Take normal precautions required when leaving a car in an unattended parking lot.

(142.6) Turn left, climbing over the metal guardrail. Scramble down the highway embankment and through the drainage, climb up the hillside and over a barbed wire fence onto a firebreak road. Go 0.3 mile up the very steep firebreak road heading to the right (south).

Note: There is no sign but this is a legal ingress to the Lower Cottonwood Creek Wildlife Area. You will soon leave the highway and noise behind as you get deeper into the open country of the wildlife area.

(142.9) Turn left at the next junction. Go 0.7 mile continuing straight up a very steep hill.

(143.6) Turn left at the junction at the first saddle. Go 0.4 mile down the hill (east) skirting around fenced cattle land.

Note: When you come to a gate on the road leave it open or closed as you found it. There may be cattle in the area.

(144.0) Pass a water-pumping windmill delivering water to a cement tub on the left. Go 0.4 mile as the road levels a bit, but continues going downhill.

(144.4) At the next fork head left and go through the gate. Go 1.2 miles passing through a riparian corridor with willows and a few huge cottonwoods.

Note: This is the only shady spot you will find on the trip so a good place to take a break.

(145.6) At the next fork stay straight. You will be heading east. Go 0.5 mile to a junction under high voltage wires.

(146.1) Turn right (south). Go 0.3 mile.

(146.4) Turn left on a faint path heading towards the O'Neill Forebay. Go 0.3 mile.

Note: If you have parked at the Lower Cottonwood Creek Wildlife Area parking lot continue straight ahead at this junction, following the high voltage wires. In 1 mile the Wildlife Area parking lot will be across the road to the left.

(146.7) Turn left on the paved road. Go 0.3 mile.

(147.0) Enter the group campground. When you reach the water's edge turn left. Go 1 mile.

Note: There are restrooms and water here.

(148.0) End at the San Luis Creek Recreation Area Campground.

road goes over the reservoir and the water blocked all the firebreak trails. It was not as bad as we had expected. The shoulder was wide and trucks sailing by gave us ample berth. Still the wind wake shook us every time one passed.

To enter the Lower Cottonwood Creek Wildlife Area we had to crawl over a guardrail, down an embankment and through a hole in a chain link fence. Then there was another a barbed wire fence to climb. This was a legal entrance to the reserve, but clearly not meant to be used. From there the hike was straight up. The sun bore down and there were no trees for relief. The flowering season is very short here because of the hot spring sunshine, but when the wildflowers bloom they can blanket a whole hillside in a single color. Even though the peak of the season had already passed we still found traces of orange poppies and blue lupine amidst the yellowing grass. At the saddle we stopped for lunch and to keep from melting in the sun we had to make a shade lean-to from our tent fly and hiking poles.

The hike was then straight down, but eventually leveled out to pass through a verdant cottonwood-lined riparian area following a small creek. It was a shady Shangri-la for us as well as for the birds that sought refuge in that cool slice of greenery. We did not see another person out there, or even any traces of their trash and that left us feeling very contented.

Cottonwood

Resources for Section Three

Maps:

Department of Fish and Game
Los Banos Wildlife Area
18110 W. Henry Miller Avenue
Los Banos, CA 93635
(209) 826-0463

Accommodations:

Casa De Fruta
10031 Pacheco Pass Hwy
Hollister, CA 95023
831-637-2666
www.casadefruta.com

Pacheco State Park
38787 Dinnosaur Point Rd.
Hollister, CA 95023
(209) 826-6283

San Luis Reservoir State
Recreation Area
31426 Gonzaga Road
Gustine, CA 95322
(209) 826-1197

Looking east over the Lower Cottonwood Creek Wildlife Area

Fishing on the old bridge near Hills Ferry

Section Four: San Joaquin Valley

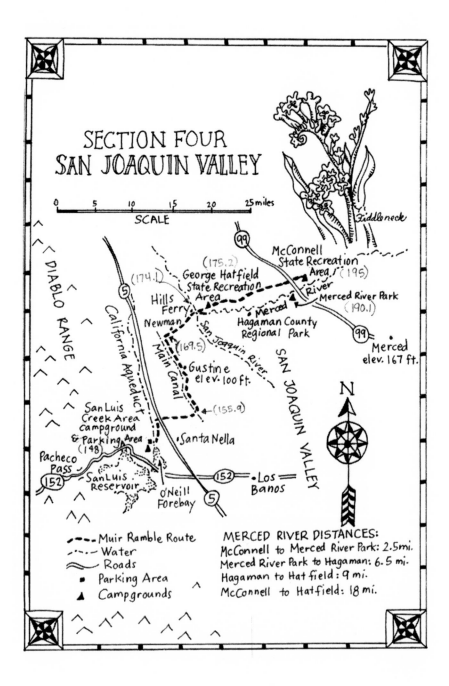

SECTION FOUR
SAN JOAQUIN VALLEY

0   5   10   15   20   25 miles
SCALE

Fiddleneck

99
McConnell
State Recreation
Area (195)
(175.2)
(174.1)
George Hatfield
State Recreation
Area
Merced
River
Merced River Park
(190.1)
Hills
Ferry
Newman
Merced
Hagaman County
Regional Park
99
Merced
elev. 167 ft.

DIABLO RANGE

California Aqueduct

5

San Joaquin River

(169.5)

Main Canal

Gustine
elev. 100 ft.

SAN JOAQUIN VALLEY

(155.9)

N

San Luis
Creek Area
campground
& Parking Area
(148)

Santa Nella

Pacheco
Pass
152
San Luis
Reservoir
152
Los
Banos

5

O'Neill
Forebay

- - - Muir Ramble Route
- · - Water
〰 Roads
■ Parking Area
▲ Campgrounds

MERCED RIVER DISTANCES:
McConnell to Merced River Park: 2.5 mi.
Merced River Park to Hagaman: 6.5 mi.
Hagaman to Hatfield: 9 mi.
McConnell to Hatfield: 18 mi.

Section Four: San Joaquin Valley

Through Hike

Begin: San Luis Creek Recreation Area Campground,
O'Neill Forebay
End: McConnell State Park, Ballico
Distance: approximately 47 miles

This section of the MRR crosses the San Joaquin Valley from the O'Neill Forebay (west of Highway 5 near Santa Nella) to Ballico (east of Highway 99 on the Merced River). The route follows the California Aquaduct Bike Trail north to Newman, then heads east to Hills Ferry where it crosses the San Joaquin River. It then continues east following a wiggling route of small roads just north of the Merced River until it passes under Highway 99 to end on the Merced near the town of Ballico.

In 1868 Muir described the San Joaquin Valley as "one vast plain divided by two rivers, the Merced and the San Joaquin." Today it is a rural farmland defined by its borders to the west and east: Highway 5 and Highway 99. In 1868 there were no dams in the foothills. Both rivers ran free and annually flooded the vast empty landscape. The Swamp Act of 1850 decreed that a man could claim all the swampland he could survey from a boat, and local legend has it that rancher Henry Miller put a boat on a wagon and after a heavy winter's rain claimed most of the "West Side" of the San Joaquin Valley. In 1870 this same Miller, needing irrigation water for his newly acquired farmland, built the first canal across the valley, from present day Millerton Reservoir to Crow's Landing, about 100 miles north. Then known as the Miller-Lux Canal and now called the Main Canal, it was completed in 1880. Today, both rivers are dammed and the San Joaquin Valley is covered with tiny towns, small dairy farms, great fields of grain and vast orchards of fruit and nut trees. It is lightly populated, and mostly flat, crisscrossed by little roads and irrigation canals so a great place to ride a bike, the MRR often follows these roads and canals to cross the valley.

Recommended Trip

Begin: San Luis Creek Recreation Area Campground, O'Neill Forebay

End: McConnell State Park, Ballico

Distance: approximately 47 miles

We have both walked and cycled across the San Joaquin Valley and currently recommend taking this section as a bike trip. We say currently because legal lodging isn't availably spaced at a reasonable day's walk. As a bike trip it can easily be done in two days. We recommend spending the night before you start the trip at the San Luis Creek Campground. The next morning begin by following the California Aqueduct's bike trail. The aqueduct is a stark cement waterway, and the bike trail is not much more picturesque, but it is elevated and thus provides expansive views over the fields of the flat San Joaquin Valley. Leave the bikeway just after passing Newman and follow rural roads to cross the Merced River at Hills Ferry, the actual spot where Muir crossed in 1868. End the day with a swim in the Merced River before setting up camp at Hatfield Recreation Area.

The next morning continue across the valley following canals and small streets past almond orchards, fields of grain and small dairies where curious Holstein cows line up along the fences to watch you pass. After crossing under Highway 99, end the day at the McConnell State Recreation Area where you can take another swim in the Merced River and then set up camp or return home.

Recommended Side Trip

In 1876 Muir floated down the Sacramento River on a raft he christened "Snag" and in 1877 he floated down the Merced River: "I built a little unpretentious successor to Snag out of some gnarled, sun-twisted fencing, launched it in the Merced opposite the village [Hopeton], and rowed down into the San Joaquin—thence down the San Joaquin past Stockton and through the tule region into the bay near Martinez. There I abandoned my boat and set off cross-lots for Mount Diablo, spent a night on the summit, and walked the next day into Oakland." [3]

If you want take a side trip in Muir's footsteps, well, really in his paddle strokes, you can take an 18 mile raft trip down the Merced River from McConnell State Park to the Hatfield Recreation Area.

The Merced River is dammed upstream, so can be quite shallow and usually runs very slowly, about a mile an hour in late spring. The river corridor is completely undeveloped and wonderfully natural, with many different species of birds and fish (a horned owl even flew close over our head as we floated by its roost). At McConnell Park there is a simple map with rafting instructions and floating distances. We took our first trip in a small rubber raft, but after that used a canoe which made the trip quicker and more pleasant. There are places to pull out or camp along the river, including the Merced River Campground at mile 2.5 and Hagaman County Park at mile 9.

The trip can be done as a loop, leaving your raft at McConnell, parking your shuttle vehicle at Hatfield, then riding your bike back to McConnell, and floating back to the shuttle vehicle. The 18 mile trip could take all day or more, and the bike ride back a few hours, so plan accordingly.

What you need and need to know

Maps:

Street maps: AAA California Regional Series map: Gold Country.

Compass Map: Merced County.

Accommodations:

There are five campgrounds and one hotel on the route.

Canals and Access Roads:

The MRR follows roads beside canals managed by three different irrigation districts, each with different policies, and these may change without notice. You will need to contact them to be sure the canal maintenance roads are currently open to the public. At the end of this section you will find information for contacting the irrigation districts.

You will see signs on the canal access roads that say "Authorized Vehicles Only" so don't drive your car on them.

The land on either side is often private property, and because of vandalism and theft, some access roads have been closed. Please be considerate: do not stray off the roads onto the private property. If you get to a locked gate or a "No Trespassing" sign just use the other side of the canal, or a nearby street.

Bicycles:

If you are cycling we recommend fat tires; ride a hybrid or mountain bike. The surfaces of the access roads are dirt and change with the passing seasons. When it makes a difference, we will recommend which side of the canal to ride on, but you will have to keep your eyes open and make your own decisions. Remember the whole trip can also be taken on the county roads that parallel the canal maintenance roads.

Section Four Trailhead Information

Through Hike Beginning Trailhead:

Access by Car: The entrance to the San Luis Creek Recreation Area is near the bottom of the pass, about 6 miles west of Highway 5, and 10 miles east of Dinosaur Point Rd. Turn east and follow the entrance road. Go 0.4 mile to an entrance kiosk. (Currently $6 for day use or $25 for overnight camping.) Go 0.5 mile. Turn left at the sign for San Luis Creek Camping. Go 2.1 miles to the campground and day use parking area.

Access by Public Transportation: Merced County Dial a Ride provides bus service from Livingston to Hilmar (TSA3), Hilmar to Gustine (TSA 10) and Gustine to Santa Nella (TSA 4). Each route makes 3 trips per day. $5 for an all day pass.

Ending Trailhead:

Access by Car: Exit Highway 99 on Collier Rd. Go east 0.2 mile. Turn left on Canal Dr. Go 1.2 miles. Stay right on South Ave. Go 1.3 miles. Turn right on Pepper St. Go 0.5 mile. Turn left on 2nd Ave. South. Go 0.5 mile. Turn right on McConnell Rd. Go 0.2 mile, to the entrance for McConnell State Park.

Access by Public Transportation: Merced Taxicab Co.

Recommended Trip Trailhead:

Same as for Through Hike.

Recommended Side Trip Beginning Trailhead:
MRR mile 195.0

Ending Trailhead:
MRR mile 175.2

Dairy cattle in the San Joaquin Valley 2006

In Muir's day the San Joaquin Valley was a vast open plain of tule-filled wetlands. Today it is sectioned out as farm and dairy land that is irrigated and drained by a crisscross series of canals. There are only the beginnings of infrastructure improvements (like the parks and bike trails that can be found in the San Francisco Bay Area) and this stymied us at first when planning our trip. Then, reading that Muir had planned to cross the valley and find Yosemite by following the Merced River, we realized we could probably do the same by following irrigation canals.

Leaving the San Luis Creek Recreation Area Campground we traced north around the O'Neill Forebay towards its outlet. The forebay is man-made, a reservoir that holds water from the California Aqueduct. Water is pumped up into the San Luis Reservoir at night when electricity is cheap then let back down into the forebay and into the aqueduct during the day to make electricity at a profit. We passed a crowd of fishermen at the aquaduct outlet, but saw no one after that as we walked the bike trail/maintenance road beside the waterway. We are still surprised at just how few people we encountered on our ramble. If our observations are true in general, then there are very few people getting outdoors in the state of California.

Section Four Directions

(148.0) Leave the campground or parking lot. Go 0.1 mile, heading east, towards the water, then turn left and follow the paved path along the shoreline.

(148.1) Go through the bike/pedestrian access gate/stile in the chain link fence and follow the service road on the west side of the California Aqueduct. Go 0.9 mile.

Note: This is beginning of the California Aqueduct Bikeway (CAB).

(149.0) Cross over the McCabe Road Bridge. Go 2.6 miles following the bikeway on the east side of the Aqueduct.

(151.6) Turn right and exit the bikeway on Butts Rd. Go 1.8 miles.

Note: Alternatively you can stay on the CAB to Newman: exit right on Orestimba Rd., turn left on Bell Rd., then rejoin the MRR at mile 169.5.

(153.4) Turn left on Whitworth Rd. Go 0.5 mile.

(153.9) Turn right on Bunker Rd. Go 2 miles, passing an unmarked canal and crossing Highway 33.

(155.9) Turn left on the western service road of the unmarked Main Canal (managed by the Central California Irrigation District). If you get to Ingomar Rd., you have gone too far. Go 5.7 miles following the canal as it generally winds its way north.

Note: Main Canal is the old Miller-Lux Canal. Check with CCID for current access policies.

(161.6) Cross over Highway 33 as the canal runs under the highway just south of Gustine. Go 7.9 miles taking the east side of the canal. You will cross several unmarked streets and private driveways as the canal winds northwards, passing the town of Newman in the distance to the east.

Biking beside Irrigation Canal in the San Joaquin Valley

Note: If you turn right on Highway 33, in 0.3 mile you will come to Gustine, with many places to get food. You can rest in the shade of Henry Miller Park at the center of town (follow 7th St. north to 3rd Ave.) You don't have to backtrack; you can get to the canal by heading north on 7th St. When 6th St. ends, turn left on North Ave./Fentem Rd. Go 1 mile and you will reach the canal and the MRR at approximately mile 162.6. Turn right.

(169.5) Leave the canal and turn right (east) on Stuhr Rd. Go 1 mile.

Note: The street sign for Stuhr is on the west side of the canal, and there is a white concrete water valve box stenciled with the word "cemetery" on the east side of the canal. Be careful on Stuhr, and watch for fast-traveling cars that may not be expecting pedestrians or cyclists.

(170.5) Cross Highway 33. Go 2 miles.

Note: To the right is The Hamlet Motel, the only motel directly on the route. It has clean reasonably-priced rooms.

(172.5) Stuhr Rd. ends. Turn left on unmarked Hills Ferry Rd. Go 1.6 miles.

Note: This is a busy road with narrow or non-existent shoulders, so be very careful.

We followed the California Aqueduct north towards the Turlock Irrigation District's Main Canal, which runs north and east across the San Joaquin Valley. We followed surface streets to connect between the two water systems and soon after we left the Aqueduct's trail we made a wrong turn. We walked over a mile before we noticed the mistake. That meant two extra miles because we had to walk back again. What irony, we never lost our way in the wilderness!

When we tell people about our trip the first thing they usually want to know is, "What was the worst thing that happened?" Some writers can get very dramatic about their troubles. We could go on and on about our heavy packs (but we are light weight packers, so can't), leaky tents (actually, we had a good tent so we stayed dry), and scary wild animals (we *did see a mean dog or two). It makes for a good story. It's true we had many uncomfortable moments. It rained almost solid for the first fourteen days straight, but we were walking in John Muir's footsteps and he always underplayed the bad. For example he had a flare up of malaria in this area and all he wrote about it was, "I had a week or two of fever before leaving the plains for Yo Semite, but it was not severe, I was only laid up three or four days..." Today any hiker who got malaria would call 911 and get airlifted straight to a hospital. Muir just continued walking.*

Gustine to Hills Ferry: (161.6 – 175.2)

The irrigation canals, like train tracks, took us to the backside of everywhere. We saw colorful ragged barns as we walked past almond orchards, dairy ranches and cultivated fields. We studied old farms like books, reading their histories from the weathered buildings and ramshackle additions. Around noon we finally reached the San Joaquin River and crossed at Hills Ferry exactly like Muir had 138 years before. Well not exactly. Muir crossed on a ferry and we used a bridge.

A monster red truck raced past us, wheels so large we could still see the horizon looking under the vehicle. The driver slammed on his brakes, spun around and stopped straight in front of us, heading right into traffic. Mirrored windows hid the driver and we worried about what we might be hassled for.

(174.1) Cross the San Joaquin River on a bridge. Go 1 mile.

Note: Hills Ferry, where Muir crossed in 1868, was a few hundred yards downstream.

(175.1) Stay left at the old arched metal fishing bridge. Hills Ferry Rd. becomes Kelley Rd., as River Rd. heads off to the right. Go 0.1 mile.

(175.2) George Hatfield State Recreation Area is on the right. Go 1.5 mile.

Note: Spend the night at the Hatfield Recreation Area if you are taking the recommended trip. The Merced River wraps around the park, and you will feel miles away from cities and highways as you swim in the river. There are beautiful camping and picnic areas nestled under mature shade trees. Locals call it Mosquito Park, so be prepared at dusk.

(176.7) Turn right on Turner Rd. Go 0.3 mile. (It becomes Mitchell Rd. at a sharp left.)

(177.0) Turn right on Swensen Rd. Go 1 mile.

(178.0) Swensen dead-ends. Turn right on Faith Home Rd. Go 0.2 mile, until it dead-ends at Turner Rd.

(178.2) Turn left onto the service road for the Stevinson Canal, which parallels Turner Rd. Go 2.1 miles.

Note: For current canal access status contact the Turlock Irrigation District (TID). The service road is sand and dirt. If you are cycling and would rather ride on pavement, you can follow an alternate route: Continue on Turner Rd. and go 3 miles. Turn left on Columbus and go 1.7 miles. Turn right on Geer Rd. and go 3.5 miles. Geer Rd. becomes Randolph Rd., go 0.5 mile. Turn right on Bloss Ave. and go 2.5 miles. Turn left on Sycamore St. and connect with the MRR at mile 190.0.

Canoeing on the Merced River in the San Joaquin Valley

(180.3) The canal veers north, and forks. Stay right, following the east fork, which is Lateral No 8. Go 4.7 miles.

(185.0) At a 90-degree right turn, the canal changes its name to the Highline Canal. Go 1 mile.

(186.0) The right (south) canal road merges with an unmarked city street, Wiliams Ave. Go 0.5 mile to Griffith Rd.

(186.5) Cross Griffith Rd. Go 1 mile, following the northern service road to Merced Ave. (The south road is closed.)

(187.5) Cross Merced Ave., turn left and then continue on the south service road. Go 2.6 miles, crossing Hinton Ave.

Note: The orchards here are peaches, and the canal road is surfaced with pits!

(190.1) Turn right on Bloss Ave. Go 0.6 mile. Bloss becomes Collier Rd. at the intersection with Campground Rd.

Note: Campground Rd. leads to the Merced River Resort, a private campground with river access, showers and full hookups.

Warning: There is no shoulder on Bloss

Maybe we were walking too close to his cows? Would this be one of those scary occurrences we could write about? When the power windows came down, the driver, a big tough-looking sort of guy stuck his head out. He yelled to us: "Are you the two walking to Yosemite? I saw the article about you in the paper. Have a great trip!"

Muir had described the landscape opposite Hills Ferry as a "flower-field" and a "sheet of flowers." That's not how it looked to us. We found miles of orchards, farmland, and smelly cattle yards. We saw few flowers except the weeds: bright yellow mustard and dandelion, white and pale yellow radish, bright purple thistles and little geranium. The only native flowers we saw were poppies and fiddlenecks. Farmers mostly hate fiddlenecks, they make cattle sick and lower the value of their harvest. We loved them; their vibrant orange color brightened our day.

It would have been easier if Muir had been an ornithologist instead of a botanist: the San Joaquin Valley is a birdwatcher's paradise. As we ate lunch and rested by the side of the road we found ourselves at the edge of the San Luis National Wildlife Refuge, a game reserve for birds. Cliff swallows, egrets, Swainson's hawks, kestrels, western meadowlarks, killdeer and turkey vultures played in the nearby wetlands. We began to notice a foul sewage smell. The local waste treatment plant was directly adjacent to the Wildlife Refuge and when the San Joaquin spilled over its banks earlier that week it flooded the waste treatment plant and flushed raw sewage into the Refuge. I could only think of how unjust it was to give the birds such an unsafe sanctuary.

Irwin to Delhi
(175.2 – 190.1)

We crossed the San Joaquin Valley, from Irwin to Delhi, on packed sand service roads beside irrigation canals. Passing a picturesque old farm building surrounded by fields of grain, we asked the farmer what he was growing. "Silage." "What?" "Silage."

Not wanting to seem ignorant we didn't ask a third time. It took awhile but we finally figured out what it was. Silage is a mixture of grains grown to feed cattle. It used to be stored in silos, hence the term, but now is stored under tarps that are held to the ground by a spider web of sliced-in-half automobile tires tied together with twine. I

Ave. and 16 wheelers use it regularly, so be careful.

(190.7) Continue on Collier. Go 0.6 mile, passing under Highway 99.

(191.3) Turn left on Canal Dr. Go 1.2 miles.

Note: In 0.5 mile you will come again to the Highline Canal as it runs parallel to Canal Rd. This is still a TID canal.

(192.5) Turn right on South Ave. Go 1.3 miles.

Note: The canal turns left in 1 mile. Leave it and follow South Ave. for 0.3 mile.

(193.8) Turn right on Pepper St. You will see a sign for McConnell State Recreation Area. Go 0.5 mile.

(194.3) Turn left. Pepper St. becomes Second Ave. Go 0.5 mile.

(194.8) Turn right. Second Ave. becomes McConnell Rd. Go 0.2 mile, to the entrance for McConnell State Park.

(195.0) End at McConnell State Park. There is a day use or camping fee.

Note: This is the end of this section and the recommended trip. McConnell State Park is a 74-acre recreation area, the first state park in the San Joaquin Valley, opened in 1950. It is named after Thomas McConnell, a sheep rancher and pioneer who homesteaded here in 1871.

The park sits on the banks of the Merced River, and four miles upstream is an ancient village site that belonged to the Northern Valley Yokuts. There are picnic, camping and play areas in the shade of mature cottonwood and sycamore trees. A short path leads to a sandy beach with a swimming hole in the river, where visitors swim, or fish for catfish, black bass and perch. You can end your trip with a cool swim in the river, then take a hot shower back in the campground (bring quarters).

Note: The recommended side trip begins here. You can talk to the park employees about where to safely leave your stuff when you float down the river.

Sycamore

decided they should start calling the stuff "Tarpage."

Delhi to Ballico
(190.1 – 199.7)

We spoke to the Delhi Historical Society. We told them how much we had enjoyed walking through the San Joaquin Valley and getting to know its history. We told them of John Muir and how his first act of conservation had been to purchase land near Hills Ferry to preserve it from development.[4] Many of our audience were farmers and they understood John Muir's motivation.

Our road map showed that the road skirts around a nine square mile chunk of private property. We thought about trying to cut through it to save miles and avoid walking with trucks, and wondered what would happen if we got caught trespassing. As we passed the first driveway into that property an old truck was driving up the road toward us. We flagged it down. More serendipity. The driver owned the ranch. He gave us the funniest look, probably because we still had on the "John Muir" costumes we wore when we gave a talk to the Delhi Historical Society. I had on an old wool vest, bowler hat, and a billowing silk cravat. Donna wore a green calico ruffled dress and flowered hat. When the rancher found out it was just the two of us he said, "No problem." When he found out what we were doing and that John Muir might have walked on his land he even let us camp the night there.

Resources for Section Four

Maps:

Compass Maps
1172 Kansas Ave.
Modesto, CA 95351
www.compass-maps.com

Transportation:

THE BUS - Merced County
Transit
880 Thornton Road
Merced, CA 95340
www.mercedthebus.com
Dial-A-Ride: (209) 384-3111

Merced Taxicab Co
2010 Yosemite Pkwy
Merced, CA 95341
(209) 722-8294

Accommodations:

Hamlet Motel
27101 State Highway 33
Newman, CA 95360
(209) 862-2845

George J. Hatfield State
Recreation Area
4394 North Kelly Road
Hilmar, CA
(209) 632-1852
www.parks.ca.gov/
?page_id=556*

Hagaman County Park 19914
W. River Road
Stevinson, CA 95374

Merced River Resort
7765 Campground Road
Delhi, CA 93315
(209) 634-6056

McConnell State Recreation Area
8800 McConnell Road
Ballico, CA 95303
(209) 394-7755
www.parks.ca.gov/
?page_id=554 *

San Luis Reservoir
State Recreation Area
31426 Gonzaga Rd.
Gustine, CA 95322
(209) 826-1197

Canal Road Access:

Turlock Irrigation District
333 East Canal Drive
Turlock, CA 95380
(209) 883-8380

Merced Irrigation District
P.O. Box 2288
Merced, CA 95344-0288
(209) 722-5761
customerservice@mid.org

Central California
Irrigation District
1717 Valeria St.
Dos Palos, CA 93620
(209) 392-3783

Painting near Twenty Hill Hollow, Snelling

Section Five: Lower Foothills

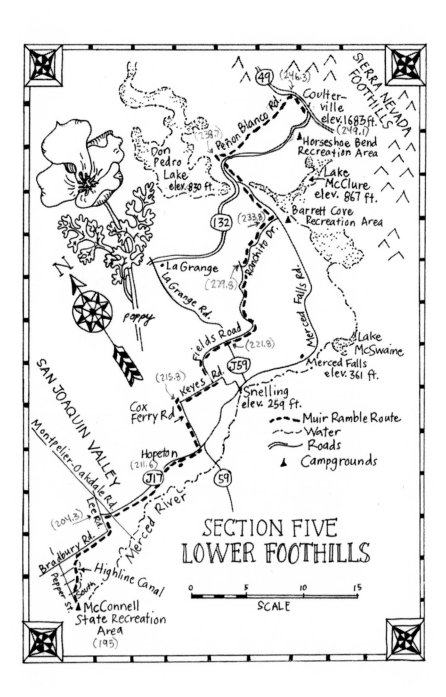

SIERRA NEVADA FOOTHILLS

49 (246.3)

Coulter-
ville
elev. 1683 ft.
(249.1)

Peñon Blanco Rd.

(239.7)

Don
Pedro
Lake
elev. 830 ft.

Horseshoe Bend
Recreation Area

Lake
McClure
elev. 867 ft.

Barrett Cove
Recreation Area

132

(233.8)

Ranchito Dr.

La Grange
(229.8)

La Grange Rd.

Merced Falls Rd.

poppy

N

Fields Road

(221.8)

Lake
McSwaine

J59

Merced Falls
elev. 361 ft.

(215.8)

Keyes Rd.

Snelling
elev. 259 ft.

Cox
Ferry Rd.

Muir Ramble Route
Water
Roads
Campgrounds

SAN JOAQUIN VALLEY

Montpelier-Oakdale Rd.

Hopeton
(211.6)

J17

59

Lee Rd.

(204.3)

Merced River

Bradbury Rd.

SECTION FIVE
LOWER FOOTHILLS

Highline Canal

Pepper St.

South

0   5   10   15

SCALE

McConnell
State Recreation
Area
(195)

Section Five: Lower Foothills

Through Hike

Begin: McConnell State Park, Ballico
End: Coulterville
Distance: approximately 54 miles

Section Five of the MRR begins near the eastern edge of the San Joaquin Valley at about sea level. The route climbs through the lower foothills and the surrounding vegetation changes gradually with the elevation gain. The trip begins following little roads past big almond orchards. Those small roads become rural truck routes as the MRR passes Hopeton. Near Snelling the route follows Fields Rd. through vast pastoral grasslands speckled with wildflowers in vernal pools and dotted with huge valley oaks. As the route circles Don Pedro Lake it gently climbs through subdivided ranch land, past oak and wildflower covered hills with tombstone rocks cropping up through the tall grass. Beyond the lake the terrain becomes more steep; brushy ceanothus, scrub oak and gray pine begin to appear. The section ends in Coulterville, at 1680 feet elevation, where tall ponderosa pines begin to scent the air with a woodsy smell.

Muir would still recognize the lower foothills: the landscape is still very rural, covered mostly by ranch and farmlands. But the region has not remained unchanged. Recently, relatively cheap land brought an invasion of commuters and exponential population growth without corresponding improvements to the county's infrastructure. The result has been that in many places there are too many cars, traveling fast, on narrow roads with narrow or non-existent shoulders. Nevertheless we had a great adventure walking through there in 2006. But given the road situation and the fact that legal lodging isn't spaced at a reasonable day's walk we can't recommend it as being very safe or fun, at least not yet.

We can however recommend the entire section as a bike trip for the strong, experienced, street savvy cyclist. It can be done leisurely in two 26-mile days, spending the first night at McConnell, the second at Barrett Cove Campground on Lake

McClure and the third in Coulterville. Because Fields Rd. is dirt, a street cyclist will have to leave the MRR at mile 212.8, follow Highway 59 to Merced Falls Rd. then rejoin the MRR at mile 233.8.

Recommended Trip

Begin: The intersection of Figmond Ave. and Fields Rd. (MRR mile 218.5)

End: The intersection of Hayward Rd. and Ranchito Dr. (MRR mile 229.8)

Distance: 11.3 miles.

The recommended trip is a very nice long day hike on Fields Rd. that begins just north of downtown Snelling, at MRR mile 218.5. The paved rural road becomes gravel and then finally becomes dirt. It is easy to imagine that this is the landscape Muir saw when he walked through. After crossing the La Grange Rd. at MRR mile 221.8 there is a gate. From there the road is closed to cars, but walking and cycling are allowed. The recommended trip ends back on rural roads at MRR mile 218.

This is a one way trip so you will need two cars or a shuttle. There is also the option to call a taxi. These are rural places so take normal precautions when parking your car for extended times. To make the trip shorter you can leave from the intersection of Fields Rd. and La Grange Rd. (J59) for an 8-mile hike. If you want to extend the trip you can turn right on Ranchito Dr., follow it 4 miles, cross Merced Falls Rd., and continue another mile to the Barrett Cove Recreation Area Campground.

What you need and need to know

Street Maps:

AAA Sectional Series: Central California

AAA Regional Series: Gold Country

Accommodations:

Hotels: There are no hotels before the B&B on Penon Blanco Rd. In Coulterville there is the Hotel Jeffery, which provided lodging and meals when Muir passed through in 1868.

Camping: There is a campground at Barrett Cove on Lake McClure and an RV campground in Coulterville.

WARNING:

The land on each side of Fields Rd. is private so do not hop the fences or stray off the road. Be considerate and "leave no trace" so that it will remain open to the public.

Section Five Trailhead Information

Through Hike Beginning Trailhead:

Access by Car: Exit Highway 99 on Collier Rd. Go east 0.2 mile. Turn left on Canal Dr. Go 1.2 miles. Stay right on South Ave. Go 1.3 miles. Turn right on Pepper St. Go 0.5 mile. Turn left on 2nd Ave. South. Go 0.5 mile. Turn right on McConnell Rd. Go 0.2 mile, to the entrance for McConnell State Park.

Access by Public Transportation: none

Ending Trailhead:

Access by Car: Follow State Highway 132 to the intersection with Highway 49 in Coulterville.

Access by Public Transportation: Mariposa County has dial-a-ride service (Mari-Go) between Coulterville and Mariposa. It runs on a very limited schedule, but you may be able to work out something with them. In the future, we hope more busses will run in Mariposa County. Sierra Taxi also runs a 24-hour taxi service.

Recommended Trip Beginning Trailhead

Access by Car: From Snelling, go north on Montgomery St. Go 2.2 miles. Turn right. Go 0.5 mile to the intersection with Figmond Ave.

Access by Public Transportation: none

Ending Trailhead:

From Snelling, drive east on Highway 59/County Rd. J16. Go 6.4 miles. Turn left on Merced Falls Rd. Go 9.2 miles. Turn left on Ranchito Dr. Go 4 miles to the intersection with Hayward Rd.

Access by Public Transportation: none

We were up just after sunrise and set out walking through the ranch. The clear sky was a radiant blue. Nature was all around us. The almonds just ready to bud and bloom. By early morning we reached the old Turlock Rd. Most of the time were able to walk on dirt roads at the edge of the orchards to stay out of traffic. We left the paved road and followed a canal service road that took us through about ten miles of almond orchards. The trees were green but the ground at the base of the trees was bare. Though composed of living trees, that ten-mile almond orchard seemed too sterile to call natural.

I became really discouraged thinking about how much we have messed with nature. I thought again of the "steel locust" and how Muir's "meadowscapes" between San Francisco and Gilroy had been bulldozed into business parks. I realized that mankind has made a trade-off, exchanging the hardships and uncertainty of living at the mercy of nature for the comforts and security of civilization. But at that moment, thinking about how our population is growing exponentially, it was hard to feel hopeful about the future. I guess Muir had similar thoughts on his walk, for at one point he wrote, "But all this beauty of life is fading year by year, fading like the glow of a sunset, foundering in the grossness of modern refinement."[5]

Section Five Directions

(195.0) Leave McConnell State Park on McConnell Rd. Go 0.2 mile.

(195.2) Turn left on Second Ave. Go 0.5 mile.

(195.7) Turn right on Pepper St. Go 0.5 mile.

(196.2) Turn left (west) on South St. Go 0.1 mile.

(196.3) Turn right on the Highline Canal maintenance road. Go 1.7 miles, crossing two streets, to Bradbury Rd.

(198.0) Turn right (east) on Bradbury Rd. Go 1.1 miles.

(199.1) Turn left on Ballico Rd. Go 0.2 mile, continuing until you cross the railroad tracks.

(199.3) Turn right on Santa Fe Dr. Go 0.4 mile.

(199.7) Make a slight left on Bradbury Rd. Go 2.6 miles.

(202.3) Turn left on Lee Rd. Go 2 miles.

(204.3) Turn right on West Turlock Rd. (County Road J17). Go 7.3 miles.

Note: Turlock Rd. was first a wagon trail between Turlock and Snelling. It is now a busy road, used by big trucks, so be careful. The miles of orchards you pass are almonds. The miles of vineyards belong to the Gallo winery. 3.7 miles from Lee Rd., there is an irrigation canal on your left. This is the Northside Canal, and it leads directly to Cox Ferry Rd. at MRR mile 214.7. The Northside Canal is managed by the Merced Irrigation District and they currently do not allow the public to use the maintenance roads for exercise or pleasure. Contact MID to ask if this has changed, and if not, make a request that they reconsider their policy.

(211.6) Pass the almost abandoned town of Hopeton. Go 1.2 miles.

Note: Muir settled near Hopeton during the summer after his 1868 trip to Yosemite, and some of his letters were mailed from its post office. At the time Hopeton was an active port on the Merced River, but after the railroad was built, and the water from the river was diverted for irrigation, river navigation became impossible and the town was deserted. Now all that remains is one house, a church and the Hopeton Elementary School. Before 1866, Hopeton had been called Forlorn Hope, perhaps because of its lack of success in gold mining, but perhaps with a premonition of its future.

(212.8) Turn left on Cox Ferry Rd. If you get to Highway 59 you have gone too far. Go 3 miles.

(215.8) Turn right on Keyes Rd. Go 0.2 mile.

Note: If you continue straight ahead on Keyes Rd., in 4.2 miles you will reach the small town of Snelling. The huge piles of river rock beside the roads and bordering the river are remnants of massive gold dredging operations from the early 20th century. If you want to learn more about this county's history and see old maps of the region, we suggest you take a side trip to Merced and visit the County Courthouse Museum.

(216.0) Turn left on Los Cerritos Rd. Go 0.5 mile.

Snelling to Fields Road near La Grange (215 – 233.8)

By the tme we reached Snelling there were low rolling hills and the landscape was no longer completely flat. It was the first time I had ever noticed how level roads are. The orchards went up and down following the natural contours of the landscape but the paved road cut straight through the undulations, rising at a constant grade. Muir's walk would have been a real meander compared to ours. The almond orchard roads led us to Fields Road, a ten-mile section of unpaved county-owned road. There are locked gates on both ends so there were no cars, no people, and no almonds. The weather was balmy, the skies were blue. A sea of wildflowers, yellow goldfields, orange fiddlenecks and white popcorn flowers, washed away the cares of the previous day. A rutted ranch road led us upwards through miles of rolling hills, grazing land for cattle, covered with wildflowers, oaks, and tombstone-like rock outcroppings. At one point the field north of the road was completely purple with vetch, lupine, clover and giant larkspur while the field to the south was brilliant yellow with butter-and-eggs, mariposa lily, monkey flower and tidy tips. We were back in Muir's California landscape.

At the end of the day we could see Snelling, Hopeton, and Ballico below us. Past them, shrouded in haze, were the San Joaquin Valley and the Diablo Range. We had walked fifteen miles. When people asked how far we walked in a day and I told them ten miles was our average, their jaws often dropped like that is some great feat. It's not. It doesn't take a John Muir kind of athlete to walk, and anyone can take up long distance walking. I did!

Fields Road to Lake McClure (233.8 – 244.8)

We found a detailed map in a real estate office that showed horse trails through a nearby subdivision called the Don Pedro Estates. The old "John Muir luck" seemed to be with us. The subdivision was vast, with custom homes on multi-acre lots, filling what a few years ago was a pastoral ranch just like the one Fields Road passes through. There were so many wildflowers I figured the real estate agents must have planted them: yellow fiddleneck, goldfields, frying pan poppy, seep-spring monkey flower, white popcorn flower, bird's eye gilia, multi-colored owl's clover, mariposa lily, and all kinds of lupine. The Estates probably seemed a thing of beauty to a real estate developer, but to us, always trying to look through John Muir's eyes, even with the profusion of wildflowers, it looked like an ecological disaster zone. The roads divided natural meadows and ran in straight lines rather than following logical contours of the landscape. Invasive non-native oleander and eucalyptus were planted to replace the native ceanothus and oaks.

(216.5) Turn right on Figmond Ave. Go 2 miles.

(218.5) Turn left on Fields Rd. Go 3.3 miles until Fields Rd. appears to end at La Grange Rd.

Note: This is the start of the recommended trip. In 1.5 miles, just before the road turns to gravel, look to the northwest and you will see a series of small hills. This is what John Muir called Twenty Hill Hollow, when he lived there as a shepherd in the winter of 1868-9. The next summer he took the sheep to high pasture in Yosemite as recorded in his book "My First Summer in the Sierra".

(221.8) Cross La Grange Rd. (County Road J59). There is a locked gate blocking an unmarked dirt road. This is a continuation of Fields Rd. that is closed to vehicle access but open to the public and pedestrians or cyclists. Climb over another locked gate. Go 6.5 miles until you reach another gate across the road.

(228.3) Climb over the gate. Go. 1.5 miles, climbing one more gate (this is where Fields Rd. becomes Hayward Rd.) and continue until you come to pavement.

(229.8) Turn right on Ranchito Dr. Go 4 miles.

Note: This is the end of the recommended trip.

(233.8) Turn left on Merced Falls Rd. Go 3.2 miles.

Note: If you cross Merced Falls Rd. and continue straight, in 1 mile you will reach the Barrett Cove Campground.

Warning: Merced Falls Rd. is a main thoroughfare and cars are driving fast, so be extra cautious.

(237.0) Turn right on Castillo Way. Go 0.9 mile.

(237.9) Turn left on Arbolada Dr. Go 0.2 mile crossing Highway 132.

(238.1) Turn right on Abeto St. Go 0.3 mile.

Almond orchards near Hopeton

(238.4) Turn right on Enebro Way. Go 0.2 mile.

(238.6) Turn left on Highway 132. Go 0.1 mile.

Note: This is a very busy road; use caution.

(238.7) Turn left on Granite Springs Rd. (this is also signed "Moccasin via Marshes Flat Road" and on some maps is Lozano St.). Go 0.9 mile.

(239.6) Turn right to stay on Granite Springs Rd. (the bigger road that continues straight ahead is Lozano St.) Go 2.2 miles.

(241.8) Turn left on Peñon Blanco Rd. Go 4.5 miles.

Note: Locals say that Muir followed Peñon Blanco with the sheep in 1869. In 3 miles, at the summit, you will pass the Lookout Bed and Breakfast on the right. As you descend the hill, looking north-east you can see the white quartz outcropping that gave Peñon Blanco its name.

Why do people move to the "country" then try to make it look like the "city"?

We followed the map searching for the horse trails. Where the trailhead should have been we found only a faint track heading off through a field of tall weeds. We followed the trail but after a short distance it disappeared. We had to cut through someone's yard to get back to the road. A sedan pulled up next to us, and the driver rolled down his window. We felt the air-conditioned cool air blast out. He said, "Saw you in the Modesto Bee. How's your trip going?" We chatted, asking if he knew any way to cut through the subdivision to get us out of there quickly.

"Nope. Want a ride?"

"No thanks."

"I guess I understand. That would be cheating. But are you sure? It's the fricking twenty-first century after all!"

Lake McClure to Coulterville
(244.8 – 249.1)

Coulterville was six and a half miles up the road and we were scheduled to give a talk for the Coulterville Historical Society just after noon, so we set out at first light hoping to avoid the heat and traffic. The road was lined with wildflowers, especially purple lupine and blooming pink clover. We could hardly believe they were native. They weren't. A roadside sign read, "Wildflowers Courtesy of Acme Construction."

We spoke to the Coulterville Historical Society. We dressed in our costumes, showed our maps and told our stories. We described walking, both for pleasure and as a way to get somewhere. We explained our idea for getting people to care about preserving local natural resources and historic landmarks: if you can just get them to visit and fall in love with them then conservation will seem desirable, logical not fanatical.

After the talk we stepped outside and gazed up at the snow-covered Sierra. The skies were beautifully clear but only two weeks before snow had been falling just above the town. Muir had encountered a snowstorm at Crane Flat, about a four-day walk from Coulterville, and we were told Crane Flat had snow now. We brought snowshoes with us but didn't really want to have to use them. We decided to lay over in Coulterville for a few days to give the sun a little more time to melt the snow.

(246.3) Peñon Blanco Rd. ends. Turn right (south) on Highway 49 towards Coulterville. Go 2.8 miles.

Note: This is also a very busy road; use caution.

(249.1) End at the intersection of Highways 49 and J132 (aka Greeley Hill Rd. and Main St.) in Coulterville.

Ponderosa Pine

Fields Road bordered by an oak-grassland landscape

Resources for Section Five

Public Transportation:

Mari-Go
Mariposa County Transit
4639 Ben Hur Road
Mariposa, CA 95338
(209) 966-7433

Sierra Taxi
5176 Hwy. 49N Ste. E
Mariposa, CA 95338
(209) 966-6781

Accommodation:

Camping info for Barrett Cove:
Merced Irrigation District
Parks Department(/
Campground Information
9090 Lake McClure Road
Snelling, CA 95369
(209) 378-2521
Camping reservations:
(800) 468-8889
www.lakemcclure.com

Coulterville RV Park
5009 Broadway Rd
Coulterville, CA 95311
(209) 878-3988

Penon Blanco Lookout B & B
4705 Penon Blanco Road
Coulterville, CA 95311-9702
www.yosemitecountry.com

Hotel Jeffery
1 Main Street
Coulterville, CA 95311
(209) 878-3471
www.yosemitegold.com/
jefferyhotel

Side Trips:

County Courthouse Museum
21st and N Streets
Merced, CA 95340
(209) 723-2401
Open Wednesday through
Sunday, 1:00 p.m. to 4:00
p.m.
www.mercedmuseum.org

Canal Road Access:

Merced Irrigation District
P.O. Box 2288
Merced, CA 95344-0288
(209) 722-5761
customerservice@mid.org

Coulterville

Section Six: Upper Foothills

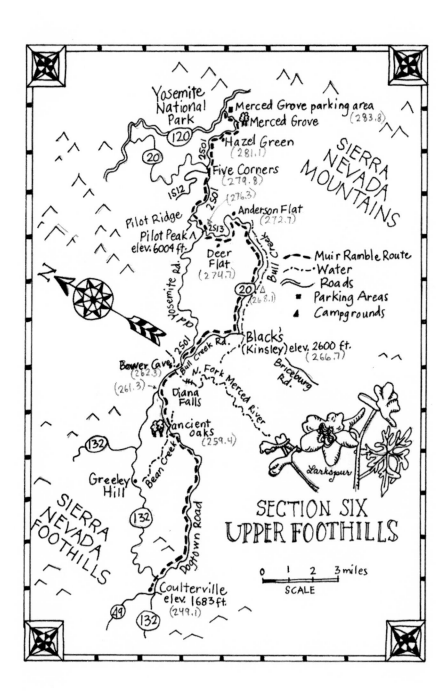

Section Six: Upper Foothills

Section Six: Upper Foothills

Through Hike

Begin: Coulterville
End: Yosemite's Merced Grove Trailhead
Distance: approximately 35 miles

Section Six of the MRR follows rural county roads through a lightly populated region of northern Mariposa County, then dirt roads through the Stanislaus National Forest and ends at the northwestern border of Yosemite National Park. The trip begins in Coulterville where old Gold Rush era buildings line the main street. Out of town the quiet of nature begins to permeate and the human footprint becomes less apparent. Few cars will pass as you wander through the shady canyon along Maxwell Creek and you will find wildflowers, newly leafing oaks and fragrant ceanothus growing at its side. As the route winds up dry chaparral-covered hills the road alternates between asphalt and gravel and occasionally reveals expansive views back to the San Joaquin Valley. The dirt Forest Service road continues to climb and drop through forests eastward towards the North Fork of the Merced River where a side trip to swim in Diana Pool may slow you down a bit. The route then passes Bower Cave, an attraction that used to be so popular that Muir mentions it. The route begins to climb again as it wanders beside Bull Creek towards Anderson Flat at 3,400 feet. It then climbs steeply through thick and fragrant stands of Yerba Santa and buckbrush past Deer Flat and on to Pilot Peak Ridge at 5,400 feet. From there the route passes Hazel Green and crosses the Yosemite Park border where the broadleaf forest gives way to mixed conifers, and the majestic sugar pine, that Muir called "King of the Forest", begins to appear. Section Six ends just past the Merced Grove of giant sequoias at the Highway 120 trailhead.

This is not High Sierra wilderness backpacking. We think of it as a backpacker's bonus region: a lower elevation trip that can be done when the high Sierra is still buried under snow. The little traveled National Forest Service land of the lower Sierra is worth getting to know. There are wildflowers, grand vistas and interesting remnants of the region's gold mining past.

Recommended Trip

Begin: Coulterville

End: Yosemite's Merced Grove Trailhead on Highway 120

Distance: approximately 35 miles

The recommended trip encompasses the entire section and can be done either as a 4-day backpack or a 2-3 day mountain bike ride. If you are backpacking the first day is an easy 10-mile walk from Coulterville to an unimproved campsite on Bean Creek, or you can go a bit further to a camp in a nearby ancient black oak grove. Day two is a 9-mile hike to a Forest Service campground on Bull Creek. The third day is a hard 11-mile hike (with 3630 feet elevation gain) to Pilot Peak Ridge at 5,400 feet where you gain vast views in all directions. Day four is a 6-mile hike to the ending trailhead on Highway 120. There is camping at the Crane Flat Campground, which is several miles down the highway but pedestrians will find there is not much of a shoulder on the road. The same itinerary can be followed on a mountain bike, or varied as your skills allow.

What you need and need to know

Park Maps:

National Forest Map: Stanislaus National Forest, Tom Harrison Maps: Yosemite National Park

Accommodations:

There are no hotels on the route, but you can camp. Camping is allowed in the National Forest by permit, which is free and can be obtained from the ranger station in Groveland. Study the camping regulations when you get your permit and follow the rules while on your trip.

Bicycles:

Bicycles are allowed on all roads and trails in the National Forest, but are only allowed on roads in Yosemite National Park. The trail from the Merced Grove to Highway 120 is considered a road, so they are allowed there, but the path down to the Merced Grove is considered a trail and bikes are not allowed there.

Water:

There is little public water available, but in the spring there will be water in most of the creeks. All stream water will need to be purified before drinking.

Remember:

Leave No Trace!

WARNING:

After heavy rainfall, be cautious at river crossings that don't have bridges.

Section Six Trailhead Information

Through Hike Beginning Trailhead:

Access by Car: Follow State Highway 132 to the intersection with Highway 49 in Coulterville.

Access by public transportation: Mariposa Public Transit, Mari-Go.

Ending Trailhead:

Access by Car: The trailhead is a turnout on the right of Highway 120, 4.5 miles east of the Big Oak Flat entrance station.

Note: The Merced Grove trailhead is not a normal trailhead for backpackers, and if you are shuttling you will have to get permission to leave a car there overnight. Get this permit from the wilderness permit station at the park entrance. Leave a note on the dashboard with your wilderness permit number on it. As of January 2010, there are no bear boxes at the trailhead. The closest bear boxes are at the Crane Flat Campground. If the campground is closed you can still find the bear boxes under the snow.

Access by Public Transportation: Yosemite Area Transportation System (YARTS) can be used to get from Yosemite Valley to Crane Flat, but there is no service while the Tioga Road is still closed and only limited service after the Tioga Road opens in the spring. Call YARTS for current routes and schedules.

Recommended Trip Trailhead:

Same as for Through Hike.

Section Six Directions

(249.1) Leave Coulterville on Main St. (also called Greeley Hill Rd. and J132) heading east, toward Yosemite. Go 0.4 mile.

(249.5) Turn right on Dogtown Rd. Go 0.2 mile.

Note: You will follow Dogtown Rd. for a total of 11.8 miles.

(249.7) Cross Maxwell Creek on a small one-lane bridge. Go 1.1 miles.

(250.8) Cross a second bridge. Go 0.9 mile.

(251.7) Dogtown becomes a dirt road. Go 2.8 miles.

(254.5) Turn left at the intersection where Schilling Rd. leaves to the right, and go downhill on the paved road. Go 0.4 mile.

Note: At this junction there is an ATV trail up the hill to the left (north/west). It leads to a small dry camping spot with an almost 360 degree view of the foothills and the Yosemite high country.

(254.9) Pass Date Flat Parking Area on the left. Go 1.7 miles.

Note: There are restrooms but no drinking water. This is a place for off-road vehicle riders to park their trailers and camping is not allowed.

(256.6) Pass Ernst Rd. on the left. Stay right. Go 1.6 miles.

(258.2) Cross Dutch Creek on a one-lane bridge, the pavement ends again. Go 1 mile.

(259.2) Cross Bean Creek (no bridge, so use caution in the rainy season). Go 0.4 mile, immediately passing a driveway

Coulterville to Greeley Hill (249.1 – 259)

Our plan had been to walk on Highway 132 to Greeley Hill, but during our layover we had learned of an alternative route that followed Dogtown Rd. What a great discovery. Dogtown Rd. was lined with oak, gray pine and wildflowers galore: popcorn flower, buttercup, Indian warrior, shooting stars, scarlet campion, lupine and the ever-present fiddleneck. It was paved for the first few miles then turned to dirt. We saw traces of mining claims and passed quaint old buildings that still lived the history of the region. "No Trespassing" and "No Hunting" signs were plastered everywhere. There were no cars.

The road was not clearly marked. We had only marginal maps so got lost a few times, but always knew we were heading in the right direction and weren't really concerned. As we gained elevation the damp woods ended and dry chaparral began. Missing an unmarked turnoff we ended up on a steep, rutted, all-terrain-vehicle trail that led us to a knoll with a stunning 360-degree view. What luck! To the west we could see all the way back to the Don Pedro Estates and marveled at the distance we had come. To the northwest was the white quartz stripe on Mt. Penon Blanco. To the east was Pilot Peak, our landmark for the next few days. Above that was the snowy Sierra and Yosemite.

on the left that looks like it might be the main road. Stay right to continue on Dogtown Rd.

Note: There is a campsite on the side of the road just before Bean Creek. In spring it is filled with blooming wild azaleas. 0.2 mile further up the road the 2S44 leaves to the left. 0.1 mile up the 2S44 you will find a dry campsite in a grove of giant black oaks.

(259.6) At the next junction, where the 2S45 goes off to the left, stay right to continue on Dogtown Rd. Go 0.3 mile.

Heritage black oaks near Greeley Hill

(259.9) Cross Bean Creek again. Go 0.5 mile.

Note: There is no bridge. In the spring of a very dry winter the water was about a foot deep, but when we walked through after a very wet winter the water was raging.

(260.4) Pass a driveway on the right that looks like it could be the main road. Stay left. Go 0.9 mile, continuing until Dogtown Rd. ends.

(261.3) Turn right on Greeley Hill Rd. Go 0.5 mile.

Note: Even though this is a main road, it is infrequently traveled and pleasant to walk.

We passed an old homestead where the road divided the property in two. I couldn't resist peaking into an open barn. There, surrounded by all sorts of machinery, tools and random bits of metal, was a rustic and rusting old sawmill. It was a primitive machine, and ancient, like the one Muir had run for Hutchings in the Yosemite Valley. Across the road we heard a lawn mower whining so went over and shouted, "halloo." Happy to stop work and chat, the fellow told us the history of the mill: Long before he was born, his grandfather moved it there from Anderson

Flat to make lumber for the neighbor's cabins. He told us stories about working the mill with his own father, sawing local ponderosa and sugar pine into rough boards and of the sparks flying when they hit nails. The mill had two circular saw blades, one above the other, each about four feet in diameter. The top one was rusty and the bottom one shiny. "We just don't get trees that big anymore..."

Greeley Hill to Black's (259 – 266.7)

We began the day walking on Greeley Hill Road and left all traffic behind when we turned onto Red Cloud Mine Road. We could see why the locals had so vehemently tried to discourage us from taking Red Cloud Mine Road. The rains had turned its red clay roadbed into liquid mush and now it had "yahoo" ruts more than a foot deep. I think they just couldn't fathom that we were *walking*, not driving, to Yosemite.

John Olmsted was walking with us. Born 100 years after Muir, in 1938, Olmsted is a botanist and historian but prefers to be known as an ecologist. In 1968 Olmsted had thought to re-walk Muir's route to Yosemite as a centenary event. He abandoned the idea as "un-Muir-like" when he realized that most of the trip would be walking on busy roads and highways. Not to be deterred in his effort to honor Muir, Olmsted set out to create a more "Muir-like" trip across California through public and private open spaces from

(261.8) Pass Buck Meadows Rd. on the left, Greeley Hill Rd. becomes Bull Creek Rd. (also called NF 20, Briceburg Rd. or N2S05) Go 0.4 mile.

(262.2) Cross the North Fork of the Merced River. Go 0.1 mile.

Note: The Diana Pool and nearby unimproved campsites are about a mile to the southwest. The trail/road leaves on the right, just before crossing the bridge. Go 1.2 miles to reach the campsites, and just beyond are the swimming holes and waterfalls. In 1856 a 20 mile wagon road was built by miners from Coulterville to Black's Station. It passed the pools, crossed the Merced River and followed Bull Creek up to Blacks. Remnants of that trail can still be found upstream of the pools hidden in the dense, almost impassable underbrush along Bull Creek.

(262.3) Pass a historical marker and Bower Cave on the left. Go 0.2 mile.

Note: The historic marker describes the Coulterville-Yosemite Road, which leaves ahead to the left as the 2S01. Completed in 1874, it was the first stage road into the Yosemite Valley. At that time it was called the Coulterville Road, but now it is known as the Old Yosemite Road. Behind the marker is the trail to Bower Cave. In the late 1800s the cave was a local hot spot, with lively socials. Today it is a home for swallows, bats and poison oak, but remnants of a dance floor and musician's platform can still be seen. The cave has religious significance for the local Me-Wuk Native Americans. In respect, access to the cave is limited and

Hotel at Black's stage stop located between Bower Cave and Anderson Flat

a permit obtained from the Groveland Ranger District is required to visit it.

(262.5) Stay right at the next "Y" junction. Go 4.2 miles, continuing on NF 20, passing a big meadow on the left signed Kowana Valley.

Note: Muir certainly would have stopped at Kowana Valley. In his day Black's stage stop was located there. With pasture for horses, a saloon and overnight lodging in the loft, it was highly recommended in travel books of the 1860s. The actual structure still exists at the east edge of the meadow, a red wooden and rock building next to the modern house. The folks who live there are history enthusiasts and may open a B&B or be willing to provide a camping spot for folks following the MRR. Contact

Mendocino to Lake Tahoe where there was still much open space. With the help of friends he created a foundation to purchase land, or right-of-ways, to connect these open spaces together. He calls that route the "Muir Restoration Trail" (www.restorecalifornia.net).

Olmsted was deliriously happy to be fulfilling his dream by finally re-walking Muir's 1968 trip, if only for a few miles. Near the junction of Red Cloud Mine and Dogtown Roads, still in National Forest land, on the border of an area filled with clear-cut pines and newly planted tree seedlings that Olmsted called "tree plantations", we found a giant black oak tree. It towered over us, huge and ancient. Looking around we found eight of them, all over 5 feet in diameter and over 75 feet tall. We lay down on the ground beneath one to rest, gazing skyward through huge gnarled limbs, tangles of smaller branches and little waving leaves, marveling at the lacy light green sheen they created overhead. John cried ecstatically, "A miniature old growth forest. These trees were here before Muir and Chilwell." Then we noticed the grove was marked with blue and yellow flags. We were not sure if the flags were meant to save them or mark them for cutting. "We have to make sure they are saved." Olmsted cried.

We rejoined Greeley Hill Road and passed Bower Cave, a small natural limestone cavern that Muir had visited, where Olmsted left us. We continued on Bull Creek Road, the "wagon road to Deer Flat" Muir mentioned in his account. And, just as Muir had recorded, the dogwood was in bloom with graceful white blossoms standing out in sharp contrast to the shady dark green forest background. Below the dogwood were rare bleeding hearts, tiny pink heart-shaped flowers, brightening the road edge. Gaining altitude the appearance of fir trees gave a clear sign that we were leaving the foothills and entering the Sierra.

Late in the afternoon we came to what was Black's Stage Stop in Muir's day, a geological bench where the last lazy stretch of Bull Creek passes through a huge meadow before falling towards the

them in advance to find if lodging is available.

(266.7) Turn left on Anderson Valley Rd. (also called the NF 20 and 2S02). Go 1.4 miles, on the north side of the creek.

Note: In 1856 George Coulter and L. H. Bunnell joined together to construct a horse trail from Black's to Yosemite. Called the Coulterville Free Trail, it followed Bull Creek to Anderson Flat, then passed through Deer Flat, Hazel Green, Crane Flat and Tamarack Flat to Yosemite Valley. In 1868 this was the main northern route to Yosemite, and Muir's description of his route makes it clear he followed the Coulterville Free Trail. Traces of the trail's rock retaining walls can still be found between the NF 20 and the creek.

(268.1) Pass a National Forest campground on the right. Go 3.8 miles.

Note: The campground has an outhouse. You can get water from Bull Creek, but will need to purify it.

Buckeye

DST

(271.9) Pass a turnout on the right, just before the road leaves the creek. Go 0.4 mile.

Note: Down the hill from the turnout are some nice swimming holes. Follow a bare granite ridge over and through the brush and poison oak down to the creek.

(272.3) Cross a gate and cattle guard. Go 0.2 mile.

Note: There are few road signs for the next 12 miles. To help avoid confusion, every intersection will be mentioned.

(272.5) Turn left on the 2S13, the next road junction. Go 0.2 mile.

Note: If you stay right on the NF 20 in 0.1 mile you will reach Anderson Valley (also known as Anderson Flat, the names are used interchangeably on maps and signs). There is a camping area with an outhouse. You can filter water from Bull Creek, which meanders through the valley, and in a dry year this may be your last source of water for the next 10 or 15 miles.

(272.7) Pass a gate. Go 0.1 mile.

Note: This is often closed to block vehicle access, especially when the roads above are muddy, but hiking is allowed even when the gates are closed.

(272.8) Pass the 2S22 on the right. Go 1.8 miles.

(274.6) Pass an unmarked road on the left. Go 0.1 mile.

(274.7) Pass another unmarked road on the left. Go 0.9 mile.

Note: Deer Flat, where Muir said the wagon road ended in a trail, is just west of here.

Merced River. For centuries before the Gold Rush this was a winter home for the Me-Wuk Indians. Today Richard and Lynn Ferry live there in an "off the grid" home. Next to their house there is an old timber, rock and red clay building that in 1868 was Black's Hotel. John Muir had most likely stayed there, and we spent the night on the dirt floor of the old building sleeping in Muir's sleepsteps. I used their computer to write accounts of our last few days and posted them to our web site. I couldn't even imagine what John Muir would have thought: after hiking twelve miles through wilderness to end up in a place where we could send an email.

Black's to Pilot Peak (266.7 – 277.6)

In his May 1869 letter to Mrs. Carr, Muir wrote, "Last May I made the trip on horseback, going by Coulterville and returning by Mariposa. A passable carriage-road reached about twelve miles beyond Coulterville; the rest of the distance to the valley was crossed only by a narrow trail." One day while Richard and Lynn were clearing brush on the steep hillside above Bull Creek they found beautiful old rockwork supporting a narrow old trail. It was too narrow for wagons, but clearly a trail, and they surmise it was part of the trail Muir mentioned: the Coulterville Free Trail. We started the day's hike by climbing a gate and walking on the trail. We could again say we had stepped exactly in Muir's footsteps, well exactly in Muir's horse's hoof steps anyway.

The road soon left the creek and climbed steeply, past Anderson Flat (where the old sawmill had come from), past Deer Flat, towards Pilot Peak. We wanted to sleep on Pilot Peak with its great views. That goal drove us on when logic said quit. It was getting dark when we finally got to the base of the peak. We still had a mile and a half to go. The raking light gave spectacular views of the snow-covered Sierra to the east. The sun set, the sky turned red, the view faded to black, the moon rose, almost full, and everything turned silver. We walked like machines.

Dead tired, we finally made it to the fire lookout, four thousand feet above Bull Creek. We were almost revived by the view, 360-degrees, luminous in moonlight. Donna stared down at her shoes and in her exhaustion they looked blue. She didn't say anything to me about it at the time because she knew they were really brown and she didn't want me to worry. Lucky we were just doing something safe and simple like walking from San Francisco to Yosemite and not something dangerous like climbing Mt. Everest.

Pilot Peak Fire Lookout to Crane Flat (277.6 – 286.7)

When we woke up the whole world was illuminated with sunrise, the serrated horizon line of the Sierra silhouetted by a peach and orange-colored sky. It was going to be hot. We could see everywhere we had walked the day before: the bright green meadows at Black's, Anderson

(275.6) Pass a well-maintained gravel road on the right. Go 0.7 mile.

Note: There is a spring 0.6 mile down this road. The next water is over 5 miles away, at Hazel Green. This could be a good place to spend the night and fill your water containers for the next day's hike.

(276.3) Pass a seasonally closed gate. In a few yards turn right on the unsigned Old Yosemite Rd. (the 2S01). Go 1.3 mile.

(277.6) Pass the 2S04 to the left at the top of the ridge. Go 0.5 mile.

Note: We recommend a side trip to Pilot Peak. The 2S04 leads to the Pilot Peak fire lookout. It is usually closed to vehicles. The views are worth the 2.8 miles round-trip walk. To the southwest, in the distance you can see the meadow at Black's and closer to Pilot Peak you can see both Anderson and Deer Flats. In the distance to the east, the snowy peaks of Yosemite form a jagged silhouette. There is a nice flat campsite here, but no restrooms or water.

(278.1) Pass the 2S25 on the left. Go 1.6 miles.

(279.7) Pass a road signed "Hardin Flat Road 6" on the left. Go 0.1 mile.

(279.8) At a major junction, known as Five Corners, take the second left, which is unmarked but according to maps is still the 2S01. Go 0.6 mile.

(280.4) Pass an unmarked dirt road on the left. Continue on the 2S02 for 0.5 mile.

(280.9) Pass a main dirt road to the left (this is the 1S11 and leads to Highway 120). Go 0.1 mile.

Fire Lookout on Pilot Peak

(281.0) Pass an unmarked road to the right. Go 0.1 mile.

(281.1) Continue straight through a gate with "No Trespassing" signs. Go 0.3 mile.

Note: Hazel Green is private property. You will be trespassing if you go off the road but the National Forest retains a right-of-way to use the road. In 0.2 mile, on the left there is a black plastic spring box. The caretakers at Hazel Green gave us permission to fill our water bottles there, so if you ask, you probably can get water there too. If it is a wet year, water can also be found ahead in a little creek near the Merced Grove trail, but if not, this is your last water source for 8 miles until you get to the Crane Flat Lookout (the lookout only has non-potable water that will need to be filtered).

(281.4) Pass Hazel Green's old

Flat and Deer Flat all surrounded by the darker green of the forest around them.

After about three miles we came to "Five Corners". We had been told about this place. It was more like six corners with a couple little ATV tracks to boot. The road signs were missing and since we had mistakenly left our best map in Greeley Hill we were not exactly sure which road to take. We had not seen anyone for twenty-four hours. As we stood there trying to decide which road to take a truck drove up one road towards us. The driver had a forest service map and confirmed our choice. Talking, we suddenly realized we had camped next to each other in the Yosemite Westlake Campground two days before. The vast wilderness all of a sudden got much smaller.

151

Hazel Green had been a stage stop on the way to Yosemite. It is now a private land holding in the Stanislaus National Forest, directly adjacent to Yosemite National Park. To the south and west the landscape is barren. The whole area had burned in the 1980s Foresta fire. Through some miracle, Hazel Green's pastoral meadow had escaped. Past Hazel Green we entered the burned landscape. The sun blazed hot. Charred and broken snags stood as sentinels above grey chaparral. Thick brush edged up on both sides of the road, arching to create a scraggly bower that caught on our backpacks then flew back in the face of whoever was behind. The brush got so thick we had to drop to our hands and knees and crawl. The old roadbed was so compacted from years of use that nothing could grow through it. Dripping sweat, raked by scratching branches, we snaked along a rabbit-sized hollow under the brush. What else could we do? Go back ten miles and then walk into Yosemite on a busy highway?

After forty-five minutes of crawling, the brush thinned and we could stand again. The burned landscape turned back into living pine forest. The dirt road was littered with little pinecones and we skidded on them like they were marbles. A sign let us know we were entering Yosemite National Park. We got in free for once, there was nowhere to pay the $20 park entry fee. We passed the Merced Grove's big trees, but didn't stop. Muir had come

buildings on the left and a newer log barn on the right. Go 0.3 mile.

(281.7) Pass through a barbed wire gate marking a boundary to a finger of Yosemite National Park. Go 1 mile.

(282.7) Stay left at the fork in the road where the 2S23Y goes right. Go 0.2 mile.

Note: There are some flat spots here where you can camp while still in the National Forest. Once in Yosemite no camping is allowed on the MRR until you reach Crane Flat Campground, near mile 289.

(282.9) Pass a sign for the Yosemite National Park boundary on the right. Climb over a locked gate. Go 0.3 mile.

(283.2) Pass the trail to the Merced Grove on the right. Go 0.6 mile.

Note: It is 1 mile down a steep trail to the Merced Grove. This infrequently visited grove of about twenty giant sequoias is quite peaceful. Their deeply fissured reddish bark creates a beautiful contrast of colors with the surrounding forest's green foliage. This grove had not been "discovered" by white man when Muir walked through, his road went almost directly from Hazel Green to Crane Flat. When the trees were "discovered" in 1871, the Coulterville Road was diverted to the south and east to give travelers a chance to visit the grove.

(283.8) End at the Merced Grove Trailhead parking area on Highway 120.

Sequoia

to see the "Big Trees" but at that time most people didn't know this grove existed. From the Merced Grove trailhead at Highway 120, a short walk west on the highway took us to the trailhead for a little used dirt road to the Rockefeller Grove, a stand of giant sugar pines. Little streams ran down the center of the roadbed. It was not long before patches of snow appeared and soon we were walking on snow. The day's hike had become a triathlon: brush-crawling, pinecone-rolling and then snow-hopping. We made it to the Crane Flat Fire Lookout just as the sun was setting. Pilot Peak Lookout was just a small dot behind us on the horizon and we had one of those hikers' moments of great satisfaction seeing just how far we had traveled.

Old Coulterville Road entrance to Yosemite National Park

Resources for Section Six

Maps:

Stanislaus National Forest
19777 Greenley Rd.
Sonora, CA 95370
(209) 532-3671
www.fs.fed.us/r5/stanislaus

Tom Harrison Maps (for Yosemite)
2 Falmouth Cove
San Rafael CA 94901
(800) 265-9090
or (415) 456-7940
www.tomharrisonmaps.com

Transportation:

Mariposa Public Transit, Mari-Go
(209) 966-5315

Yosemite Area Regional Transportation System (YARTS)
1-877-98-YARTS
1-877-989-2787
www.YARTS.com

Accommodations:

Kowana Valley: (Black's)
kowanalynn@yahoo.com.
theferrys@yahoo.com

Hotel Jeffery
1 Main St.
Coulterville, CA 95311
(209) 878-3471
www.yosemitegold.com/jefferyhotel

Contacts:

National Forest Ranger Station:
Groveland Ranger District
24525 Highway 120
Groveland, CA 95321
(209) 962-7825
www.fs.fed.us/r5/stanislaus

Yosemite National Park
(209) 372-0200
www.nps.gov/yose/

Visitor Center in the Valley
(209) 372-0299

Books:

Trails and Tales of Yosemite and the Central Sierra
by Sharon Giacomazzi
Bored Feet Press, 2004

The Big Oak Flat Road
by Irene D. Paden and Margaret E. Schlichtmann
Ahwahnee Press: 1955

Crossing Fireplace Creek on final descent into Yosemite Valley

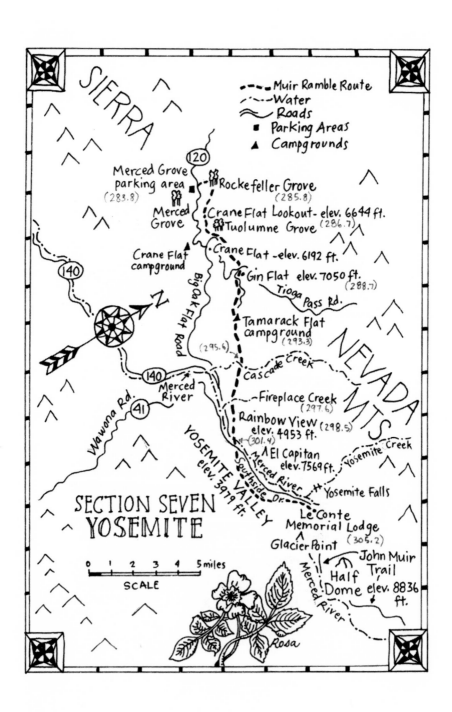

Muir Ramble Route
Water
Roads
Parking Areas
Campgrounds

SIERRA

NEVADA MTS.

(120)

Merced Grove
parking area
(283.8)

Rockefeller Grove
(285.8)

Merced Grove

Crane Flat Lookout- elev. 6644 ft.
Tuolumne Grove (286.7)

Crane Flat
campground

Crane Flat -elev. 6192 ft.

(140)

Gin Flat elev. 7050 ft.
(288.7)

Big Oak Flat Road

Tioga Pass Rd.

Tamarack Flat
campground
(293.3)

(295.6)

Cascade Creek

(140)

Merced River

Fireplace Creek
(297.6)

Wawona Rd.

(41)

Rainbow View (298.5)
elev. 4953 ft.
(301.4)

El Capitan
elev. 7569 ft.

Yosemite Creek

YOSEMITE VALLEY
elev. 3979 ft.

Merced River

Southside Dr.

Yosemite Falls

SECTION SEVEN
YOSEMITE

Le Conte
Memorial Lodge
(305.2)

Glacier Point

0 1 2 3 4 5 miles
SCALE

John Muir
Trail

Half
Dome elev. 8836
ft.

Merced River

Rosa

Section Seven: Yosemite

Section Seven: Yosemite

Through Hike

Begin: Yosemite's Merced Grove Trailhead
End: Le Conte Memorial Lodge, Yosemite Valley
Distance: 21 miles

Section Seven of the MRR follows little-used trails from Crane Flat to the Yosemite Valley floor, closely tracing the actual route Muir used in 1868. The trip starts at the Merced Grove trailhead then follows an abandoned dirt road through the Rockefeller Grove's many magnificent old growth giant sugar pines. The route climbs past the Crane Flat fire lookout then drops back down to Crane Flat near the Tuolumne Grove. From there the route runs parallel to the Tioga Rd. following Gin Flat Rd. This dirt road, now closed to vehicular traffic, provided access to Tuolumne Meadows before the current Tioga Rd. was built. In 1868 it was the route of the Coulterville Free Trail, which Muir followed. At Gin Flat the MRR crosses the Tioga Rd. and follows a paved remnant of the Big Oak Flat Rd., which here followed the route of the Coulterville Free Trail down to the Tamarack Flat Campground.

Once through the campground, the road is closed to vehicular traffic but continues as a trail. This is where Muir said that because of snow he lost the trail but found it again near "the brow of the valley." The descent into Yosemite Valley is stupendous, dramatic and strenuous. The trail is high on the north wall, directly opposite Bridalveil Fall, and to the west of El Capitan's broad face, so for most people the views of the valley will be new and wonderful. You will have to scramble across talus fields filled with boulders the size of refrigerators, but the opportunity to see El Capitan, Half Dome and Bridalveil Fall from this new vantage point will make it worthwhile. The MRR reaches the valley floor near the base of El Capitan. You can end the trip there or continue on trails past Camp Four, Yosemite Falls and Yosemite Village, to the Le Conte Memorial Lodge, the Sierra Club's home in the Yosemite Valley. This is the official ending place for the MRR, where you can sign into the "Ramble" logbook and document your trip.

Recommended Trip

Begin: Yosemite's Merced Grove Trailhead
End: Le Conte Memorial Lodge, Yosemite Valley
Distance: 21 miles

The recommended trip encompasses the whole section and can be done as a two-day backpack trip. Day one is a 9.5-mile hike. If you leave the Merced Grove trailhead by mid-morning you will be able to reach Tamarack Flat with sufficient time to set up camp before dark. Day two is an 11-mile hike that will take a full day. We have hiked this section of the MRR several times and it has always proved an enticingly beautiful trip.

The best time of year for the trip is late spring. If you leave after the snow has melted, but before the Tioga Rd. opens, there won't be any cars on the road and you will have the whole Tamarack Flat campground to yourself! But be prepared to spend a day slogging through slushy snow at the higher altitudes near Gin Flat.

This trip will require having two vehicles, except in the summer months when you can use the Yosemite Area Regional Transportation System (YARTS). If you want to cut four miles off the second day you can park your shuttle vehicle at the climbers parking area near the base of El Capitan at MRR mile 301.2.

What you need and need to know

Street Maps:

AAA Recreation Series: Sierra Nevada – Yosemite Area

Topographic Maps:

Tom Harrison Maps: Yosemite National Park

Accommodations:

Hotels: There are no hotels on the route until you reach the Yosemite Valley where there are many options.

Camping: There are campgrounds in Yosemite, and the ones on the MRR are described in the text. If you plan to camp outside of a campground you will need a wilderness camping permit, acquired at a Yosemite Wilderness Permit Station, either at the Big Oak Flat entrance station or the Valley Visitor Center.

Wilderness camping is not allowed within 1 mile of a road or trailhead. Study and follow all the camping regulations that come with the permit.

Bicycles:

Wheeled vehicles of any kind are not allowed on trails in Yosemite National Park. This section cannot be done on a bike as all of the non-paved trails the MRR follows are considered trails.

Water:

All stream water will need to be purified before drinking. There is water at the Crane Flat Lookout, but the water is not guaranteed potable and you will need to purify it. There is also water at Crane Flat Gas Station and the Yosemite Institute. The next source is Tamarack Creek, 7.5 miles away.

WARNING:

In spring the creeks will be cold and in places will be flooding over the trail. Be careful when walking through fast moving water.

If you leave a car parked anywhere in Yosemite National Park, or when camping, you are required to store all your food and scented items (like lip balm) in bear boxes or bear-proof canisters. Bear canisters can be rented from the wilderness office. Bear boxes are located at many trailheads, but not yet at the beginning trailhead for this section of the MRR.

Section Seven Trailhead Information

Through Hike Beginning Trailhead:

Access by Car: The Merced Grove trailhead is a turnout on the south side of Highway 120, 4.5 miles east of Yosemite's Big Oak Flat entrance station.

Note: This is not a standard place for backpackers to leave a car so get permission to leave your car here from a ranger at a wilderness permit station. Leave a note on the dashboard with your wilderness permit number on it. As of January 2010, there were not bear boxes at the Merced Grove trailhead. You can use the bear boxes in the Crane Flat Campground or the ones at the ending trailhead on the El Capitan Cutoff.

Access by Public Transportation: The Merced Grove Trailhead cannot be accessed by public transportation at this time, so it is easiest to do the trip with a two car shuttle system, leaving one at the beginning trailhead and the other at the ending trail head, spending the nights before and after the trip at any of the campgrounds or hotels in the valley, which can easily be reached from the ending trailhead using the free Yosemite Valley Shuttle System.

Ending Trailhead:

Access by Car: Follow road signs towards Curry Village. The Le Conte Memorial Lodge is on Southside Dr., across the street from Housekeeping, at shuttle bus stop #12.

Note: You cannot park overnight in the Le Conte parking lot, but you can use the backpacker's parking lot near Curry Village. You will need a permit, acquired from one of the wilderness permit stations, to leave your car there overnight.

Access by Public Transportation: YARTS and the Yosemite Valley Shuttle Bus.

Alternate Ending Trailhead: If you want to cut a few miles off the end of the trip, you can park one shuttle vehicle at the El Capitan climbers parking area (near MRR mile 301), which is just east of the junction of the El Capitan Cutoff and Northside Drive. There are bear boxes on the side of the road, and the Valley Shuttle Bus stops near here too.

Recommended Trip Trailhead:

Same as for Through Hike.

Shuttling suggestion:

If you are walking or only have one car, from June through September you can get from the Valley to Crane Flat using YARTS, the Tuolumne Meadows Tour Bus or the VIA Bus Service. They all leave from the Valley Visitor Center.

From Crane Flat you then have several options. You can walk from Crane Flat 0.2 mile east on the Tioga Rd./Highway 120 and join the MRR at mile 288.1, or you can walk 0.2 mile west on Highway 120 to the Crane Flat campground. If it is late you could sleep there for an early start the next morning. The road to the Crane Flat fire lookout is across the highway and 0.4

mile west of the campground entrance. You can walk 1.4 miles up the Lookout Road to visit the lookout and to continue on the Ramble at MRR mile 286.8.

Crane Flat

Crane Flat to near Cascade Creek (286.7 – 295.2)

The sun was shining and the air was crisp, the kind of air Muir tasted in the Santa Clara Valley. We now understood what Muir meant when he claimed the air "possessed of so vast a capacity for happiness". We passed Crane Flat. It was only a big snow-patched marshy meadow and we no longer worried about needing our snowshoes. Walking up the Tioga Road, looking for the Gin Flat cutoff, we came to "Road Closed" barriers. We boldly continued and no sooner had we passed the sign, a ranger truck came barreling down the mountain road toward us. The timing was a fluke, but more "Muir" luck. It was the supervising ranger for the Tuolumne area and he had recently skied from Yosemite to Crane Flat using the same route we planned to walk. He told us that at higher elevations there was still lots of snow and warned us all the rivers were high, but that we could probably make all the crossings without getting wet over our waist. We weren't sure if he was trying to encourage or discourage us.

We walked up the empty Tioga Road to Gin Flat where we found the Tamarack Flat turn off buried in snow. Only the tip of a stop sign indicated the way and the road was only a vague trace through the winter-white mountainous landscape. Route-finding took all of Donna's skills. She surveyed the topographic

Section Seven Directions

(283.8) Leave the Merced Grove Trailhead heading west on Highway 120 (back towards the Big Oak Flat entrance), walk a few yards, cross the highway, climb over, or around, a gate blocking a dirt road that heads north. Go 2 miles, following the dirt road up the hill.

Note: This is the Rockefeller Grove Trail. It is used as a winter ski route and occasionally you will find it marked with yellow or orange metal tags nailed to tree trunks about 10 feet from the ground. The road follows an old railroad bed and passes through the Rockefeller Grove of giant sugar pines. This grove is not a compact group of trees like the Merced Grove's Sequoias. It has many magnificent trees spread out over a great area.

(285.8) Turn right (east) on an unsigned trail that leads to the Crane Flat Fire Lookout. Go 0.1 mile.

Note: If the road ends you have gone 0.2 mile too far. We suggest you visit the end of the road as a detour because this 0.2 mile is lined by many of the grove's giant sugar pines.

(285.9) Turn right at the next "Y". Go 0.8 mile, heading uphill in a southeast direction, following pink and orange plastic ribbons tied to tree branches that mark a ski trail, skirting around a prescribed burn area, looking for the trail that rings the Crane Flat lookout tower.

Note: In 2008 the right fork of the Y appeared totally blocked with downed trees, and quite faint.

(286.7) Turn left on the ring trail. Go 0.1 mile.

Note: The paved area beside the lookout is used by emergency and fire fighting vehicles. It is all off limits and should never be walked across. To visit the Crane Flat Fire Lookout, take a detour and turn right. Go 0.1 mile. Turn left on the path up to the lookout. The old lookout building is no longer used for fire fighting purposes and visitors are welcome. There are stunning 360-degree views from its walkways and inside the building there are panoramic photographs captioned with the names of all the peaks.

(286.8) Turn right. Go 0.7 mile, crossing the parking lot and following the unsigned paved road down the hill.

Note: If you go 1.5 mile down this road you will come to Highway 120 and a walking entrance to the Crane Flat Campground.

Snow on the Rockefeller Grove trail

(287.5) Turn left on a dirt road (marked as a ski trail, with yellow metal ski trail marker flags nailed about 15 feet up the trees). Go 0.5 mile.

(288.0) Turn right on the service road coming from the Tuolumne Grove parking lot. Go 50 feet.

Note: If you continue straight ahead you will find the trail to the Tuolumne Grove on your left. A side trip to see these giant trees will add an extra 2 miles (round trip) to your hike. There are about twenty-five giant trees in the grove, including the famous tunnel map and then the landscape, searching for the contours that the road should follow. She watched for old blazes on trees and also for the openings above and between the trees. We didn't really need snowshoes, but we post-holed into the snow a few inches with each step, so it was hard hiking.

Tamarack Flat campground was buried in snow, so we kept going, hoping to find a wilderness campsite without snow at a lower elevation. We crossed Tamarack Creek, rushing and waist high, without even getting splashed by walking over a big fallen tree. Well, Donna walked. I was so worn out by that time that I crawled on hands and knees. We followed the snow-covered road through sugar pine and incense cedar forests down to Cascade Creek where we found a dry place to sleep on a huge granite boulder.

Cascade Creek to Yosemite Valley
(295.2 - 305.2)

Snow was soon a thing of the past and finding the trail was no longer a challenge. The Old Big Oak Flat Rd. was in relatively good condition considering it has been abandoned since the 1940s. We crossed the main fork of Cascade Creek on an old bridge. On a knoll above the bridge we found a campsite and wished we did not have a schedule to keep (we were giving a presentation about our walk at the visitors center the

tree. In days gone by cars following the Big Oak Flat Rd. could drive right through this tree.

(288.0) Turn right on a dirt road that parallels the Tioga Rd. Go 0.1 mile, until the road sweeps to the right, then cut left down the embankment and cross the Tioga Rd.

(288.1) Enter the meadow. Go about 300 feet, walking cross-country along the southern edge of this meadow, looking on the right for a yellow ski trail flag on a tree.

Note: Please be careful not to damage the meadow. If it seems too marshy, as it can be in early spring after a wet winter, walk up the Tioga Road instead. Go 0.6 mile, pass the Yosemite Institute on the left, then meet the MRR at Gin Flat Rd. (MRR mile 288.7).

(288.2) Turn right. Go 0.1 mile, following the flags through the trees to a clearing.

(288.3) Turn left. Go 0.1 mile, generally eastward, following the flags along this clearing heading to the edge of a big meadow.

(288.4) Turn left. Go 0.1 mile, following the flags around the west side of this meadow, staying left of the rocks and right of the next tree with a flag.

(288.5) Enter the trees again. Go 0.2 mile, following flags up to the Tioga Rd.

(288.7) Turn right, go 50 feet, cross the road onto an unsigned dirt road. Go 1.8 miles until you once again come to the Tioga Rd.

Note: This is Gin Flat Rd., called

Crossing the high water of Tamarack Creek.

Gentry's Rd. by some old-timers. Before the Tioga Rd. was built this was the route of the Old Big Oak Flat Rd., and before that of the Coulterville Free Trail. It climbs through a mixed conifer forest and in 1.7 miles passes the high point of the entire MRR, a rocky knoll at about 7060 feet.

(290.5) Cross the Tioga Rd. Go 2.8 miles, following the Tamarack Flat Rd. to the campground.

Note: This is where Muir lost the trail in the snow. If snow is obscuring the paved road, study your maps and geological features carefully. We found it helpful to look up towards the treetops to find the clearings that indicated the path of the road. This road is also the Old Big Oak Flat Rd. It was used as the northern entrance to the valley from 1874 until it was replaced in 1940 by the lower Big Oak Flat Rd. that is currently in use.

(293.3) Pass through the campground. Go 0.1 mile.

Note: The Tamarack Flat campground is a good place to spend the night. If it is still closed for the winter, you will need a wilderness permit. There are bear boxes and outhouses, but the only water is from the creek, which must be purified before drinking. If Tamarack Creek is flooding the road, cross upstream on a log.

next night) so could not spend a few days in this river-song sounding, pine tree-smelling, sunlit wilderness.

Below the junction with the El Capitan Trail, the Old Big Oak Flat Rd. is no longer maintained by the park service, even as a trail, and years of fallen trees blocked our path. Perhaps it would be more accurate to say they made our hike into an obstacle course. We crawled under the higher trees and over the ones near the ground, with dead branches constantly grabbing at our backpacks. I started counting the downed trees but gave up after I got to one hundred.

We lost elevation. The vegetation alternated between mixed conifer forests where the partially shaded trail was covered with long brown ponderosa needles, and hot dusty chaparral zones of mostly manzanita and ceanothus brush with an occasional black oak offering shade. We passed a series of beautifully crafted old rock walls that were built back in the 1870s to hold the road in place on the steep hillside. They were still there and still doing their job. Rounding a corner we broke out of the trees at a precipice called "Rainbow View". An old metal railing still stood there to keep us from falling over the edge as we stared across the valley at Bridalveil Fall, raging with spring snow melt. It is no wonder that early visitors wrote with such lavish praise about the beauty of Bridalveil Fall: from

(293.4) Climb over the locked gate. Go 1.8 miles, following the unmaintained continuation of the Old Big Oak Flat Rd.

Note: The sign posted here states that El Capitan is 8.4 miles and Yosemite Valley is 16.2 miles. The MRR follows a different route to the valley, so it is only 8 miles from here to the valley floor near the base of El Capitan, but they are going to be hard miles!

(295.2) Cross a fork of Cascade Creek. Go 0.2 mile.

Note: If the trail is flooded, cross on a big log just upstream.

(295.4) Pass the Foresta Trail leading to the Big Oak Flat Rd. on the right. Go 0.2 mile.

(295.6) Cross Cascade Creek on an old wooden bridge. Go 0.5 mile.

Note: There are deep swimming holes hidden from view upstream and a nice campsite on the east side of the creek.

(296.1) Pass the trail to El Capitan on the left. Go 1.5 miles.

Note: Past this point you may encounter downed trees blocking the road. In 0.3 mile you will pass the spot where Colonel E. S. Gentry built a sawmill and stage stop on the brink of the cliffs overlooking the Merced River Canyon. It served as the last stage stop before reaching the valley. In 1868, just below Gentry's was "Oh My! Point", which gave travelers their first majestic view of Yosemite Valley.

(297.6) Cross Fireplace Creek. Go 0.9 mile.

Note: The creek has eroded away the road, but it is usually possible to wade

Bridalveil Fall

through. In a dry year this will be the last water before reaching Ribbon Creek, over 3 hard miles ahead.

(298.5) Pass an old scenic view site on your right. Go 0.1 mile.

Note: This breathtaking vista is called Rainbow View. There is an old metal railing there to keep visitors, distracted by the stunning view of Bridalveil Fall, from tumbling over the precipice.

(298.6) The road ends in a field of boulders. Go 0.3 mile.

Note: Directly ahead is a remnant of rock retaining wall, part of a series of switchbacks on the Old Big Oak Flat Rd. called the 'Zigzags'. Below that rock wall is a clump of trees. The old road continues just below those trees. Traverse diagonally towards the trees then circle around

this vantage point it can be seen better than from anywhere else in the valley. Mesmerized, we watched the water pour from its source in the valley above, over the smooth lip of granite, then fall in a graceful curtain of sparkling droplets to crash as a misty bellow of spray on the rocks below.

Our route continued down the steep north slope at the west end of Yosemite Valley. Rockslides had obliterated sections of the Old Big Oak Flat Rd. and we had to scramble across sliding granite and climb giant boulders that blocked and buried what was left of the road. At one point the trail crossed a sheer granite face. Blocking our way was a dead tree stump swarming with giant black and yellow carpenter bees and it was surrounded by poison oak. We could just imagine John Muir lobbying Mother Nature to give us more challenges.

The constantly changing views of Bridalveil Fall were breathtaking and it could be seen almost all the way to the valley floor. The Old Big Oak Flat Rd. enters the valley west of El Capitan, at Ribbon Creek. We arrived sweaty and hot, and imagining what John Muir would do, splashed in Ribbon Creek, baptizing ourselves in its icy waters to celebrate our arrival. Then, to officially end our trip, we made our way to the LeConte Memorial Lodge, the Sierra Club's home in Yosemite Valley. With its visitor center full of Muir's books and a staff of nature-loving, outdoor-active volunteer docents, it seemed a fitting place to end our journey. Bonnie Gisel, the lodge's curator, John Olmsted and a few others were there to congratulate us on completing our Trans-California Ramble and to officially welcome us to Yosemite. They witnessed as we paid homage to John Muir for

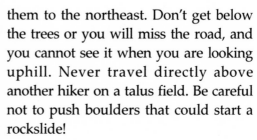

them to the northeast. Don't get below the trees or you will miss the road, and you cannot see it when you are looking uphill. Never travel directly above another hiker on a talus field. Be careful not to push boulders that could start a rockslide!

(298.9) Continue on the intermittent road down towards the valley. Go 1.2 miles, finally passing through the "wood lot" where the park service stores and cuts firewood for use at campfire programs.

Note: As you lose elevation, the views of Yosemite Valley grow in grandeur. El Capitan comes into view and Half Dome looms in the background. Bridalveil Fall is directly across the Valley and the pool above the fall can be seen spilling its contents over the brink. In spring you will find a profusion of wildflowers.

(300.1) When the road cuts back to the right, leave the road and continue straight on an unmarked trail crossing Ribbon Creek. Go 1 mile, skirting the base of the cliffs towards Yosemite Village.

Note: If you reach paved Northside Dr., you have missed the unmarked trail.

(301.1) Turn right on a wide dirt trail that climbers use to haul their gear between the base of El Capitan and their parked cars. Go 0.1 mile

(301.2) Turn left on Northside Dr. Go 0.2 mile.

Note: This is the location of the alternative trailhead at the parking area for El Capitan climbers.

(301.4) Veer right on El Capitan Crossover, the connector road between

Northside and Southside Dr. Go 0.3 mile.

(301.7) Turn left on Southside Drive. Go 0.2 mile heading east

(301.9) Turn right, off the road on a connector trail that leads to the main trail around the Valley floor. Go 0.1 mile.

(302.0) Turn left on the main trail around the Valley floor. Go 3.2 miles.

(305.2) End at the Le Conte Memorial Lodge.

Note: There is a "Muir Ramble Route" logbook in the library to sign and document your trip.

To the tune of "Oh Susannah"

Chorus:
Oh, Mr. John Muir
You saved Yosemite
For all the people to enjoy
For all eternity.
  Verse one:
Oh he came from Portage, Wisconsin
Though Scottish born was he
He traveled through the wilderness
The plant-life for to see.
He rambled over Canada
One thousand miles to the sea
Then to California
To see Yosemite.
  (Chorus)
  Verse two:
From old New York, to Panama
To Frisco sailed he
Alameda, San Jose
Then down to Gilroy(ee).
Went o'er Pacheco with its flowers
And crossed at Hills Ferry
Hopeton, Snelling, Coulterville
Then to Yosemite.
  (Chorus)
  Verse three:
I had a dream the other night
When everything was still
Dreamed I saw old John Muir
Coming o'er the hill.
A plant press was on his back
A tear was in his eye
Said I saw Yosemite
How could I help but cry?
  (Chorus)
  Second Chorus:
Oh Mr. John Muir
Your life inspired us
We've walked up to Yosemite
Next time we'll take the bus!

Resources for Section Seven

Maps:

Tom Harrison Maps
2 Falmouth Cove
San Rafael CA 94901
(800) 265-9090
(415) 456-7940
www.tomharrisonmaps.com

Transportation:

YARTS (Yosemite Area Regional
Transportation System)
1-877-989-2787
www.YARTS.com

Tuolumne Meadows Tour
(209) 372 4386
www.yosemitepark.com/
activities

VIA Adventures
300 Grogan Ave
Merced, CA 95341
(209) 384-1315
1800 VIA-LINE
www.via-adventures.com

Accommodations:

Camping reservations in
Yosemite:
(877) 444-6777
www.recreation.gov

Hotel reservations in
Yosemite:
(866) 875-8456
www.nationalparkreservations.com/
yosemite

Contacts:

LeConte Memorial Lodge
Curator
P.O. Box 755
Yosemite, CA 95389
(209) 372-4542
Email:
leconte.curator@sierraclub.org

Rockslide on the Old Big Oak Flat Road

The end of the Muir Ramble Route: LeConte Memorial Lodge

Part Four:
Conclusions - Walking is "Green"

When John Muir lost his fight to save Hetch Hetchy Valley there seemed to be very few people in the world who were concerned about the environment and the planet's ecological health. Muir's great loss may have been our greatest gain, for it raised world-wide awareness of the need to preserve wilderness.

Over the past several years, as we have walked and biked the MRR, we have thought a lot about what we can do to help preserve California's natural places. We have to confess it has been easy to feel insignificant and wonder how we could have any real effect. But John Muir's legacy proves that one person can actually have a huge impact.

In "Living Green" Jordan Ruben wrote: "we live in a world where population is multiplying, natural resources are becoming scarce and evidence of our damage to the planet is mounting…It is up to us to create a healthy environment for ourselves and those we love…by living green you can begin to be a part of the solution, through your practical everyday actions."[1]

Walking is one of these actions. Riding a bike is another. The reason they are solutions is pretty straightforward: when you walk or ride you are not polluting. Walking and cycling are simple things to do that can have profound impacts. When you walk, you reduce the congestion on roads, and therefore reduce the need to build more roads. When you bike to work instead of driving, you don't use gas or drip oil or antifreeze on the ground and you don't require another parking space be created and paved. When you walk or cycle you become a stronger and healthier person, and therefore less of a burden on your friends and society. You have the opportunity to spend more of your day outside, experiencing and enjoying the beauty of the world, as well as the opportunity to meet other human beings, rather than spending your commute time isolated inside a little metal box.

Walking the MRR as your next vacation

There is an inspiring website (www.sfbaywalk.com) created by a man who challenged himself to walk the complete San Francisco Bay Trail. On his site he writes: "In this modern era, almost nobody has walked from the San Francisco Bay Area to the Central Valley, or even thinks about doing it, so it is hard for us to imagine just how difficult it really is. I'm not talking about the difficulty of walking (although that's not that easy). I'm talking about how the motor vehicle has confiscated all the routes. In 2006, a couple walked from S.F. Bay to Yosemite. They had to do a multi-day backpack through Henry Coe State Park just to bypass the freeways. The bicyclists are well aware of the problem and have formed effective advocacy groups. Pedestrians, and there are very few of us, are at the bottom of the food-chain. These days, when I hear about somebody who has walked across the country or done some other great walking achievement, I no longer marvel at the amount of walking, I marvel at the research, planning and logistics it took to figure out how to do it."

Now that this book has been published by Poetic Matrix Press, walking the MRR to Yosemite will no longer be so impossible. The instructions and directions we give in this book take care of the planning and research, and the notes provide solutions for most of the logistical challenges. Instead of flying to a distant 'somewhere' for an exotic adventure, now, following the MRR as an exotic adventure can be one of the practical green actions you can take to make the world a better place. And if you need to fly to California to follow the MRR we have a green challenge for you: build up your own personal credits during the year before you take the trip - walk, ride a bike or use public transportation when you would have driven a car, dry your clothes on a line instead of using a dryer, eat local food from a farmers market - then redeem those credits when you take your flight to California.

Some things you can do

Here are some things you can do to help promote the MRR, the creation of more off-road routes, and safe access for pedestrians and cyclists on existing roads: Call your local mayors or board of supervisors and request the development of more walking routes in your home towns. Think globally but act locally, plan these trails so they can later be linked together to create longer trail networks. Stay aware of the political issues regarding bicycle and pedestrian routes and take every opportunity to speak out to your elected officials. Take part in or create community events that draw attention to the need to keep walking and cycling routes open, such as National Trails Day sponsored every spring by the National Hiking Society. Share the joys of walking and cycling with your friends and family and try to inspire others to leave their cars behind. Invite them to join you, at least challenge them to try self-transportation once. The more people who understand the joys and challenges of self-transportation, the more people there will be who understand the need for changes and support those changes with their money and votes.

Finally, we suggest you take the opportunity to read other books by John Muir or other adventure writers who have shared their personal experiences while walking or cycling in nature. These stories can inspire you do things you would never imagine. We know this from experience. It was reading Muir's writings that inspired us to spend the last four years of our lives creating the MRR for you to follow.

American Hiking Society
1422 Fenwick Lane
Silver Spring, MD 20910
Phone: (800) 972-8608
www.americanhiking.org

League of American Bicyclists
1612 K Street NW, Suite 800
Washington, DC 20006-2850
(202) 822-1333
www.bikeleague.org

Footnotes

Introduction:

1. Muir was accompanied on this trip by a "young English-man" who subsequently left no historical trail. In Muir's 1872 magazine article, *Rambles of a Botanist,* he never names this Englishman. In the later unpublished *Pelican Bay Manuscript* Muir names his companion "Chilwell". In this account Muir also calls him a "Cockney". The first mention of Chilwell having a first or last name is found in T. H. Watkins' *John Muir's America* (1976). In an unfootnoted passage Watkins calls him Joseph Chilwell. Subsequent writers have followed Watkins' lead but after exhaustive research we could find no documentary evidence to justify this.

2. ROB p. 767. See Footnote 3 for Part One.

3. Snyder, Gary, The Practice of the Wild: Essays.

(San Francisco, CA: North Point Press, 1990.), page 122.

Part One: John Muir's First Trip to Yosemite

1. See footnote 3. LAL p. 155.

2. See footnote 3. YOS p. 3.

3. Following are the literary sources for the text of Muir's first trip to Yosemite with the abbreviations we have assigned them:

LTD: Letter to David Muir (Muir's brother), March 1868.

LTM: Letter to the Moore and Merrill families (Friends from Indiana), July 1868.

LTA: Letter to Ann Galloway (Muir's sister), August 1868.

LTCF: Letter to Jeanne Carr, (Friend and mentor from Wisconsin) February 1869.

LTCJ: Letter to Jeanne Carr, July 1868.

LTCM: Letter to Jeanne Carr, May 1869.

LTCN: Letter to Jeanne Carr, November 1868.

PBM: The Pelican Bay Manuscript. Transcribed oral history:

Dictated and transcribed in 1907 at Pelican Bay, Klamath Lake, Oregon. Part of this manuscript became the *Story of my Boyhood and Youth*.

ROB: John Muir. Rambles of a Botanist Among the Plants and Climates of California. *Old and New*. Volume V. January 1872 to July, 1872.

TNP: John Muir. The National Parks and Forest Reservations. Proceedings of the Meeting of the Sierra Club held November 23, 1895. *The Sierra Club Bulletin*. 1:6. May, 1896.

MFS: *My First Summer in the Sierra*. John Muir. (Boston: Houghton Mifflin Co., 1911).

YOS: *The Yosemite*. John Muir. (New York: The Century Company, 1912).

TMW: *A Thousand-Mile Walk to the Gulf*. Written by John Muir, edited by William Frederic Badè. (Boston: Houghton Mifflin Co., 1916).

LAL: *The Life and Letters of John Muir*. Edited by William Frederic Badè. (Boston: Houghton Mifflin Co., 1924).

4. LTM

5. LTM, LTCJ, LTA

6. YOS p. 4.

7. LTD, LTM, LTCJ

8. LTD

9. In 1868 there was a fare war between steamer lines. First class fares dropped from $400-500 in 1867 to $150 in 1868. Muir says his steerage class ticket was about $40. (A contemporary traveler to California, John Olmsted states in his book *A trip to California in 1868* that steerage was $45.)

10. As Bade explains in TMW, the Nebraska had left on her maiden voyage around Cape Horn in January of 1868. Muir took the Santiago de Cuba to Aspinwall and connected with the northward-bound Nebraska on the Pacific side of Panama.

11. TMW, LTD

12. A "pocket map" is a small folding map. It is likely Muir had either *Bancroft's Map of California, Nevada, Utah and Arizona* (H. H. Bancroft and Co., San Francisco) or *A new map of the States of California and Nevada* by Leander Ransom and A. J.

Doolittle (W. Holt, San Francisco). Both maps show mountain ranges, rivers, cities, and major roads, but neither map has the detailed information of a modern street or topographic map, nor do they show a route from Pacheco Pass to Yosemite via Hills Ferry.

13. Muir used the plant press to preserve botanical samples. It was about 12 by 18 inches, made with strips of a strong stable wood like white oak, nailed together in a lattice. In Muir's day botanists used straw board and newspaper in place of today's corrugated cardboard and blotters. Muir once wrote a letter to his sister on narrow strips of newspaper, saying he had forgotten his writing paper and was using paper torn from the empty margins of the paper in his plant press.

An India rubber bag was the 1868 version of a dry bag/backpack. It was made out of rubber, or latex, from India, which at the time was commonly used for waterproofing.

14. TMW p. 186.

15. TMW p. 186.

16. TMW p. 186.

17. TMW p. 188, LAL p. 178, PBM p. 258-259, YOS p. 4, LTCJ.

18. The winter of 1867-1868, with a total of 38.84 inches for the season, is still the fourth rainiest year on record for San Francisco. Most of the rain fell in December and January. It even snowed in San Francisco in January. Records in the National Archives in San Bruno, California show it rained lightly on April 3 and 7, heavily on April 9-12, lightly April 13-15, and then did not rain again until May 13, when only 0.01 inches fell.

The winter of 2006, when we took our first trip on the MRR, had similar heavy rainfall with a total of 38.4 inches. It also rained the first two weeks of April and there was snow in San Francisco in January.

Newspapers editorials helped to complete a picture of the weather Muir experienced:

Mariposa Mail, March 30, 1868, THE WEATHER. – For the last few days we have been favored with clear, beautiful, balmy spring weather, and there appears to be no doubt that the snow storm on Sunday night, the 22d inst., closed the winter, so far at least, as this section is concerned. Though a friend, writing from the snow regions of the upper hills, says, "The storm-king still reigns supreme in the mountains.

Mariposa Mail, April 17, 1868, "STORMS. Our late predictions of coming good weather didn't hold. At least the good weather didn't hold. The MAIL went to press last Thursday night [Apr 9th] in the midst of a very decided storm of rain, wind, thunder and lightning. Friday [Apr 10] gave us a continuance of the storm with redoubled fury, and the addition of sleet, snow, hail, and everything else that the angry elements could send to the earth.

Mariposa Mail, May 15, 1868, COULTERVILLE. - We have already had visitors to the Yo Semite Valley this season ... On their return I joined them, and we journeyed by the old Coulterville trail over Crane's Flat. There was some snow for nearly five miles out, and it was so compact that we rode over it without any difficulty, and arrived safely, at Black's.

19. ROB p. 767, LAL p. 178, PBM p. 259.

20. LAL p. 179, YOS p. 4.

21. LAL p. 179.

22. LAL p. 179.

23. ROB p. 768.

24. TMW p. 189, ROB p. 768.

25. TMW p. 189, ROB p. 768.

26. PBM p. 259, TMW p. 189.

27. LAL p. 180.

28. ROB p. 769, LAL p. 180, TMW p. 189.

29. TMW p. 190.

30. ROB p. 769, LAL p. 181.

31. YOS p. 5.

32. ROB p. 769, TMW p. 191.

33. We understand this to mean that if "Florida" was the name one should give to a place that is "the land of flowers" then the San Joaquin Valley should be called Florida.

34. TMW p. 191, LTM.

35. ROB p. 770, PBM p. 261.

36. ROB p. 770, LAL p. 181, LTM.

37. ROB p. 770-771.

38. ROB p. 770-771, LTCJ, LTM.

39. ROB p. 771, LTCJ, LTM.

40. East of Hills Ferry, Muir separated from his English companion. In ROB Muir implies they rejoined, stating "...ere we were ready to recommence our trip..." In PBM Muir states, "This part of my journey I accompanied by a young Englishman by the name of Chilwell..." This implies the earlier English companion may have been a different person. This is also the first time the name Chilwell is used.

41. PBM p. 262, LAL p. 182, LTD.

42. ROB p.771, LTCN.

43. LAL p.182.

44. LAL p.183.

45. LAL p.183.

46. LAL p.183.

47. Muir rode a horse on his trip. The fact is verified in his May 16th, 1869 letter to Mrs. Carr. Muir wrote: "Last May I made the trip on horseback, going by Coulterville and returning by Mariposa. A passable carriage-road reached about twelve miles beyond Coulterville; the rest of the distance to the valley was crossed only by a narrow trail." In 1868 most tourists hired a guide and rented a horse in Coulterville. Muir mentions purchasing supplies in Coulterville but does not make it clear if that is where he got the horse.

48. LAL p. 184, ROB p. 771, LTCN.

49. LAL p. 184, ROB p. 771.

50. TNP, ROB p. 772, YOS p. 99.

51. LAL p. 185.

52. LAL p. 185.

53. LAL p. 185.

54. ROB p. 772, LTCN.

55. PBM p. 262, LAL p. 185, LTCM.

56. LAL p. 185.

57. LAL p. 186.

58. LAL p. 187.

59. LAL p. 187.

60. This $3 refers to the money he spent while in the Yosemite region, not on the whole trip, as it could not include the costs he incurred in Coulterville to rent a horse and buy a gun. In his May 1869 letter to Mrs. Carr, Muir writes: "Here is, I think, a fair estimate of the cost of the round trip from Stockton, allowing, say, ten days from time of departure from Mariposa till arrival at same point. Stage fare and way expenses to and from Mariposa, say $40.00; saddle horse, $20.00; provisions, cooking utensils, etc., $15.00; total, direct expense for one person, $75.00. Each additional day spent in the valley would cost about $3.00."

61. LAL p. 188.

62. LTM, LTCJ

Part Two: Creating the Muir Ramble Route

1. We needed to know if Muir used the existing roads or if he traveled through wilderness. To help answer this we needed to know what supplies Muir carried with him and if he camped out. The answers were not to be found in the account of his 1868 trip but we did find them in the account of his 1867 walk from Indiana to Florida. Muir states he carried very little: a New Testament Bible, a plant press, an India rubber bag containing a change of underwear and a pocket map of California. He did not carry much extra food and often went hungry. We found that Muir had promised his mother he would not sleep out-of-doors if he could avoid it. He wrote, "I began thus early to seek a lodging for the night." (TMW p.20) He did, however, record spending nights sleeping out. "Slept in the barrens at the side of a log. Suffered from cold and was drenched with dew." (TMW p.110) With little room in his bag and his custom of taking lodging, we began to assume that Muir might have left roads to botanize, but returned to them often, at least to get food. We also decided that Muir probably did spend many nights under the stars, but he would have found lodging when available, especially with all the rain he had on the trip.

In his account (ROB) Muir states he traveled "paying very little compliance to roads or times..." But, in the same passage, he also wrote he traveled "by any road that we chanced to find..." In 1868 the California landscape was mostly uncharted, the terrain rough and uneven, often covered by impassable brush or blocked by swollen streams. Muir did have a map with him, but it wasn't like a modern topographic map. The maps available in 1868 were all equally vague in detail, showing only mountain ranges, river drainages and the few major roads. After much consideration we determined that even if Muir traveled cross-country to botanize he would have used roads to go any great distance. Without roads, given the total mileage, his trip would have taken much longer than six weeks.

2. For more on this route see: Howard R. Cooley, Reflections on Muir's 1868 Walk from Oakland to Gilroy / A study in literature and environment. The John Muir Newsletter (Stockton, Ca.: John Muir Center for Regional Studies, University of the Pacific), V. 18, N. 2, Spring 2008, p. 1, 5-10.

3. ROB p. 770.

4. ROB p. 770.

5. LTD

6. LAL p. 185.

7. PBM

8. ROB p. 767.

9. As an example, William Brewer wrote, "The weather is perfectly heavenly. They say this is a fair specimen of winter here...warm, balmy, not hot, clear, bracing... In the yards are many flowers we see only in house cultivation [back east]: various kinds of geraniums growing of immense size, dew plant growing like a weed, acacia, fuchsia, etc, growing in the open air in the gardens..." *Up and Down California in 1860-1864: The Journal of William H. Brewer.* William H. Brewer. (Berkeley: University of California Press, 1975) Fourth Edition, p. 9.

Part Three: Guidebook to the Muir Ramble Route

1. Melville Best Anderson, The Conversation of John Muir. *American Museum Journal.* March 1915.

2. Maria L. La Ganga, "Stanford grad student walking 320 miles in John Muir's footsteps", *Los Angeles Times* (May 9, 2009) p. 1.

3. *John of the Mountains: The Unpublished Journals of John Muir*. Linnie M. Wolfe. (Boston: Houghton Mifflin & Company, 1938), p. 241.

4. TNP "Next, I tried to save a quarter-section of the flowery San Joaquin plain when it began to be plowed for farms; but this scheme also failed, as the fence around it could not be kept up without constant watching, night and day."

5. ROB p. 770. I assumed the ground was bare because it had been poisoned. I later learned that chemical use is strictly regulated for production farming. And what was I thinking anyway? If those farmers were not growing my almonds, where would my almonds come from? Some foreign country? With no environmental regulations? It is way better, for the environment, the "plant people" and the animals, that this land is used for agriculture than the alternative of having it divided by roads and converted to housing tracts or golf courses or business parks.

Part Four: Conclusions - Walking is Green

1. Jordan Rubin, foreword to *Living Green: A Practical Guide to Simple Sustainability*. Gregory T. Horn (Topanga, CA: Freedom Press, 2006), p. 7.

Index

CPSIA information can be obtained at www.ICGtesting.com
Printed in the USA
BVOW070305310812

299175BV00003B/3/P